GAME COOKERY

GAME COOKERY

IN AMERICA AND EUROPE

by

RAYMOND R. CAMP

Drawings by Richard Harrington

HPBooks

Published by HPBooks
A division of Price Stern Sloan
360 North La Cienega Boulevard
Los Angeles, California 90048

Printed in U.S.A. First Printing

by Wild Duck Press, Inc. ©1983
Reprinted by arrangement with Wild Duck Press, Inc.

Camp, Raymond R. (Raymond Russell), b. 1908.
  Game cookery in America and Europe.
  Originally published, 1983.
  Includes index.
  1. Cookery (Game) 2. Title.
 TX751.C3 1988   641.6'91   88-5239
 ISBN 0-89586-695-1

Designed by Helen Barrow

This edition is dedicated to
Pierre, Shamus and Bullet:
To the good times and good meals we've shared,
and the ones still to come.

Preface

IN 1958 I RESPONDED *to an ad in* The Wall Street Journal *for* Game Cookery in America and Europe *by Raymond R. Camp. It was, without a doubt, one of the best investments I ever made. Since then my friends and I have enjoyed many splendid game dinners prepared from the recipes in this book. Often, sharing these dishes led to new friendships and to hunting and fishing trips in Canada, Mexico, Europe and Morocco. Rarely did I find food to equal that in the unique assortment of recipes collected by Mr. Camp in the course of his travels. It seemed a shame to have this excellent book out of print, so I decided to make it available again.*

Cooking fads come and go, but this book remains a constant: a celebration of the challenge of hunting and the fine food a successful day can produce. Like the French adage, "Add lots of love and lots of butter," it is not concerned with calories, moderation or abstinence, only with quality in the preparation of each dish.

Mr. Camp must have been a most creative and enthusiastic sportsman because the anecdotes which precede each recipe reveal a man who enjoyed good food, good friends and fine hunting throughout much of the world. Times, of course, have changed; some places mentioned may no longer exist. Do not worry about that, just enjoy the recipes their kitchens produced and the good times evoked.

I have deliberately left the original text intact. It is very charming, and Mr. Camp's solid, practical cooking advice is timeless. Updating the wine chapter, for example, to include new wineries would serve no real purpose. Most good cooks today have developed their own preferences in wines to accompany game dishes, and, in any case, are not afraid to experiment.

Bringing this book back into print has been both exciting and challenging. My sincere thanks go to those most responsible for the success of this project: Sally Abell and Katharine Lunenfeld, whose creativity and perserverance caused the book to be published; Helen Barrow, who provided invaluable advice and guidance; Rick Harrington, who executed the fine black-and-white drawings throughout the book. My thanks, also, to Mrs. Raymond R. Camp for her cooperation.

Game Cookery *is a guide to enjoying some of the bounty nature can provide. I have used and enjoyed it for twenty-five years, and I wish at least as much for all of you.*

RANDOLPH A. MARKS

Contents

Foreword

THE FOLLOWING PARAGRAPHS constitute an introduction, foreword, and preface — but not an apology — to the contents of this book. None of the recipes contained herein are new and untried. They are, in every instance, methods of game preparation that have been "tried by fire." Having enjoyed them when prepared by others, I prepared them myself, tried them on others, and found them good.

From an early age I enjoyed good food and was fortunate enough to be a member of a family with similar tastes. As a small boy I lived in the center of what might be termed a "family island." My maternal grandparents, a great-grandparent, and an uncle all lived within a 200-yard radius of my own home. As the dinner hour approached I often made a routine tour of kitchens, and the menu of the day determined the table selected for the evening. There were occasions, I'm afraid, when I dropped in on as many as two or even three tables. None of the family could understand why I was such a *thin* youngster. Perhaps it could be attributed to the distance between tables.

Not long after my arrival in New York, in the late twenties, I was thrown in contact with a group of men to whom good food had become a serious hobby. This was fortunate, for it meant I could enjoy one really fine dinner each week, which otherwise would have been outside my financial grasp. This group was known as the Gourmet and Wine Club, and my election undoubtedly was speeded up by the fact that one of the original fourteen had moved to the West Coast, and some members hesitated to sit down with thirteen at the table.

Initially, each member had contributed fifty dollars to a "club fund." With this backlog a two-room-and-bath apartment was rented in the Village. Our clubrooms comprised one large room, approximately 20 by 35, a large kitchen, and a bath. The fund was sufficient to provide a long table with eighteen chairs, and to rebuild and fully equip the large kitchen.

Each month a member was assessed a few dollars for rent, upkeep, and the food and wine provided at the weekly dinner. Six members were assigned each week to prepare the Thursday night dinner. A roster was kept to provide insurance against any bickering as to who should prepare each course. You were informed of the course for which you would be responsibile a week in advance, and the sum you would be allowed under the club budget. It was amazing how much could be done for so little, but I'm afraid many of us atoned for the low budget from our own pockets.

The Gourmet and Wine Club was disbanded during World War II, and although a few of us tried to revive it later, some members had moved away and others had died, so these efforts were unsuccessful.

A number of the recipes in this book had their source in this club. All of those I have included were repeated many times by popular demand, so I consider they have passed the acid test.

There is a sound reason for my particular interest in game cookery. For almost twenty years I conducted the "Wood, Field and Stream" column in *The New York Times*. During this period I hunted and fished over most of North America, Europe and Africa. When, in the course of these travels, I enjoyed an unusually palatable dish, I would work my way into the kitchen and obtain the recipe. In many instances I was able to watch the step-by-step preparation of the dish. Thus, over many years, I found I had assembled an imposing number of recipes.

The mere possession of these recipes, however, did not inspire me to compile a book on the subject. In a sense, the decision to do this sprang from what might be termed the "crusading spirit." It has long been apparent to me that, despite the tremendous amount of game harvested in this country each year, the knowledge as to the proper preparation of this game was very slight. Too often game arrived in the kitchen without proper care, handling, or curing, and emerged *from* the kitchen minus the essential flavor and texture it should have possessed. The average cook, not excluding a number of professionals, prepared game in the same manner as he or she prepared the flesh of domestic meats. Unfortunately, perhaps one piece of game out of one thousand can be prepared with such indifference.

Game, in almost every instance, requires special preparation. The wild bird and animal leads a more active life and seldom has access to the abundance of food available to domestic creatures. Therefore, it is normally possessed of more muscle and less fat. The poultry you buy from your butcher, for example, has approximately 25 per cent of its dressed weight in fatty tissue. The wild bird rarely passes the 5 per cent mark. The same is true, in a smaller percentage, of the various forms of venison when compared to domestic beef, pork, lamb or veal.

It is essential, in the preparation of game, to find some substitute for the lack of natural fat. Unless you recognize this, and compensate for it, the result is certain to be a dry, tough and stringy portion of meat, from which most of the natural flavor has been lost through improper preparation and overcooking. Overcooking can be as harmful as underlarding.

R.R.C.

1
Waterfowl

WITH THE possible exception of venison, the average amateur chef commits more culinary crimes in the preparation of waterfowl than in any other form of game cookery. No item of game can be quite as dry, tough, tasteless and unsavory as an *over*cooked duck or goose. By the same token, few meats can charm the taste buds as forcefully as either of these game birds when properly prepared.

The duck has inspired some of the great chefs of history to ambrosial peaks rarely attained, even by members of this august brotherhood. Not all of the fine recipes that have evolved since Cleopatra tempted Anthony with Nile teal are complicated and elaborate. Some are extremely simple, but they call for reasonable attention to detail and timing.

In the preparation of *wild* waterfowl many cooks ignore the quite

15

apparent fact that these birds possess but a small percentage of the fatty tissue that swathes the domestic duck or goose. As one old duck-hunting guide put it — "There ain't enough fat on a duck to baste a snipe." Recognize this fact and accept it, and you have made the first long step in the direction of waterfowl cookery. Buy a larding needle and learn how to use it.

It is equally important to use the *right* thing in larding game. I know of a number of amateur game cooks who have developed a "secret" method of overcoming the lack of natural fat in various forms of game. They lard *all* of their game meats with bacon. While this method is satisfactory in the preparation of some game, the very flavor on the bacon itself robs the essential flavor of some of these meats. The larding material must be suited to the game, not the reverse. Some game calls for bacon, some for salt pork, some for suet, some for beef back fat, some for sweet butter, some for olive oil. The more delicate the flavor of a game bird or animal, the greater care it requires in the selection of the larding material.

The very utensils in which meat is prepared play an important part in conserving, enhancing or emphasizing the flavor. Certain methods of preparation, in which certain herbs, seasonings or sauces are employed, require that the vessel itself contribute no additional flavor. The iron or aluminum skillet that is adequate for frying or roasting may serve as an unwanted catalyst when used for stewing the same meat or cooking it in a sauce. For this reason, the earthenware pot or casserole is important in the preparation of certain dishes. You may have noticed that certain dishes you prepare have what might be described as a "metallic" flavor. Prepare the same dish in an earthenware vessel and you will note the difference. For those who are concerned with preparing food in the finest possible manner, these things are important.

I have included brief chapters on herbs, wines and sauces because these matters are extremely important to the proper preparation of food. Seasoning should enhance the natural flavor of game, not smother it, and both herbs and wine, used in moderation, can accomplish amazing things with any dish. Once you try them and learn the bare rudiments of their use, you will never be without them.

In brief, my purpose in compiling this book — for I did not *write* it, in the full meaning of the term — was to provide simple instruction in the proper preparation of game, and to offer a sufficiently wide assortment of recipes for each type of game to insure a pleasant variation of menu. For the benefit of the *amateur* amateur, the methods have been simplified, and each step of preparation is presented in what might be termed "baby English."

Many of the recipes and methods set down in these pages can be applied to domestic meats as well as game, so the scope of the book is not as limited as might be supposed from the title. It is one of the few books I have done that has been a truly pleasant task. As I went over the many recipes I renewed in my mind old friendships and memorable events. I hope it will prove to you that the proper preparation of game can be a rewarding adventure.

Canvasback McAlpin

Requirements

2 canvasbacks (mallard,
    black duck or pintail)
1 medium onion
1 carrot
⅛ pound of butter
1 lemon
1 wineglass of dry sherry
½ teaspoon of dry
    tarragon
1 bunch of green celery
salt
freshly ground pepper
1 wineglass Marsala
4 thin strips, half-inch, of
    fat salt pork

This recipe came from the Chesapeake Bay duck-hunting lodge of "Tony" Townsend McAlpin, and has been reduced in proportions to serve two normal appetites. Even a dainty eater will manage to dispose of one entire duck prepared in this manner, and the more robust the trencherman, the more glances will be cast at the plate of his (or her) companion, in hopes that an assist may be in order—just to avoid waste, of course.

During the entire period of preparation, the McAlpin's local cook croons tender spirituals in a low contralto. While this incantation may soothe the waiting and hungry hunter, it is not necessarily a requirement in the preparation of the birds. As four hungry wildfowlers had spent a good part of the day inhaling the chilled, invigorating December air that swept the margins of the Nanticoke, a bonus portion of a half-duck each was prepared.

HOW TO COOK

Stuff each duck with the following—grate carrot and onion, add tarragon and merge with celery (chopped in two-inch lengths) leaves and all. Lard each breast with strip of salt pork, working larding needle a half-inch under the skin from front to rear. Rub skin with salt and pepper. Brush each duck thoroughly with the following mixture: ⅛ pound of melted butter, juice of one lemon and one wineglass of sherry. Place ducks in shallow roasting pan in oven that has been preheated to 400 degrees, basting frequently with butter-lemon-sherry mixture, and cook for exactly twenty minutes. Place ducks on a hot platter and return to the oven. To the juices in the roasting pan add one wineglass of Marsala and merge thoroughly. Pour resulting gravy over birds. Serve with wild rice, a green vegetable, and a crisp hearts of lettuce salad with a tart dressing. Also, if you happen to have a bottle of Tavel that has been slightly chilled, you will find it serves as a perfect complement.

Ted Mulliken of Saybrook, Connecticut, not only makes the finest waterfowl decoys in the world, but is a *big* man who not only likes to cook but takes a genuine pleasure in eating the ducks he shoots over his own decoys. There is only one fault with Ted's personal method of preparing duck North Cove Style. He likes his birds a bit too rare for my taste. Instead of basting them five or six times, at three-minute intervals, he bastes them only twice at two-minute intervals, which gives him a hell of a head start on the Burgundy. However, as he usually provides both the ducks *and* the Burgundy, I have never been in a sound position to protest.

HOW TO COOK

Split the four ducks down the spine and open up until carcass is flat (pound under board if necessary). Melt in a saucepan ¼ pound butter, add the juice of two lemons, and two jiggers of applejack. (The cook and his helper then each drink one jigger of applejack.) Lightly salt and pepper the ducks on both sides, baste liberally with the butter-lemon-applejack, and *preferably* place on a charcoal grill four inches from coals. If this is not available, preheat the broiler for fifteen minutes, and place ducks under broiler, four inches from the flame. Turn and baste ducks every two minutes until they are done to taste. Preferably, they should be cut into sections with poultry shears and eaten with the fingers, along with hot garlic rolls (see recipe), a green salad, shoestring potatoes. The Burgundy should be consumed at the rate of one bottle per two ducks. Mulliken adds crisp green onions (scallions) to the bill of fare.

North Cove Black Duck

Requirements
4 black ducks
       (no substitute
       recommended)
2 lemons
¼ pound of butter
4 jiggers of applejack
       (Calvados *can* be
       substituted)
salt
freshly ground black
       pepper
two quarts of sound
       Burgundy

Mallard
Waidmanns,
Hunter Style

There is an elderly inn not far from Münster (in Western Germany) whose host, in conformity with tradition, supervises the preparation of the dishes for which the hostelry enjoys deserved fame. I found only one disappointment at this inn. My request for a bit of local "Münster" cheese was received with elevated eyebrows and a questioning stare. Münster, I learned, was justifiably renowned for many things, but cheese was not among them. It might be admitted that I was surprised, but not disappointed, at the early pre-hunt breakfast that was served to eight of us shortly after six that morning. My host, Berthold Beitz, of Essen, believed in arriving at a hunt breakfast early with the result that only one other *Waidmann* had preceeded us.

As we advanced to the snapping fire on the wide hearth his arm swept upward in a traditional hunter's salute, accompanied by a resounding *"Waidmanns Heil!"* As if by magic, at these words, an aproned waiter appeared with three small glasses of schnapps. These were downed with a deep bow all around, and we sat down to a steaming bowl of chicken broth with dumplings. After a few sips we were called to our feet by the arrival of another hunter. More schnapps all around. Another sip or two of broth, another hunter — more schnapps. One by one our group attained the final score of eight. I seemed to be the only member of the group who felt any effect from the extremely strong chicken broth.

Late that afternoon, after a dozen "drives," which produced a tall mound of hares and pheasants, we returned to the welcome fire of the inn, and more schnapps. As I had been promised one of the dishes that made the inn famous, Mallard, Hunter Style, I absorbed my schnapps in careful, well-spaced sips. The dish, accompanied by a half-dozen vegetables, including golden fried potatoes, large green beans, and sauerkraut, more than deserved its fame.

It took considerable persuasion, through the medium of an interpreter, to persuade the host to part with the recipe for Mallard Waidmanns, but he gave in when it was pointed out that I had no idea of opening a competing hostelry and would be returning to America within a week.

HOW TO COOK

Stuff each duck with the following: in a large mixing bowl place the half-head of cabbage shredded *fine*, onions shredded fine, grated carrots, dill and savory. Chop until merged. Add the yolk of one egg, ⅛ pound of melted butter, 1 wineglass of sherry, tablespoon of Worcestershire sauce, salt and pepper, and merge thoroughly with wooden spoon, finally adding one cup of breadcrumbs. After ducks have been stuffed, rub each bird with salt and pepper, cover each breast with two strips of bacon, and place in an oven preheated to 350 degrees. Baste frequently with a blend of ⅛ pound of melted butter merged with four ounces of white wine (keep basting hot). Cook for thirty minutes.

Requirements

2 mallard ducks
  (black duck,
  canvasback or pintail)
3 medium onions
½ head of cabbage
½ teaspoon ground dill
½ teaspoon powdered
  savory
4 strips of fat bacon
2 carrots
1 egg
1 tablespoon
  Worcestershire sauce
¼ pound of butter
4 ounces of dry white wine
1 cup of breadcrumbs
1 wineglass of sherry
salt
freshly ground black
  pepper

Pressed Duck

There is something of a controversy along the banks of the Seine as to the origin of the elaborate but delightful dish known as (very freely translated) Pressed Duck. You will find the same dish, variously prepared, under a dozen names.

The amateur chef who is possessed of a sense of showmanship, the sum of $40* with which with to purchase a duck press, and a cultivated palate, will be unable to resist the preparation of this dish in the presence of a small group of kindred spirits. Personally I would not consider a guest list of more than three persons. Too much work is involved.

To carry out the preparation in proper form two chafing dishes, one eight-inch and one twelve-inch, with alcohol burners, are essential. While these items are available in every good restaurant, not too many homes have one, let alone two.

Not even a lukewarm gourmet would consider departing Paris without having sampled pressed duck in a least one of its several forms. The general opinion is that the Tour d'Argent (with or without a seat at a window overlooking the River) excels in the preparation or *presentation* of this dish. Personally, I have tried it at three or four less pretentious and far less expensive (and cozier) restaurants and found it equally good. Pressed duck is one of the most rewarding of the "complicated" methods of preparing duck, but it is within the grasp of any amateur who can follow directions.

Although I have collected at least a half-dozen varied recipes for pressed duck, the one I prefer came from the prized "cooking notes" of a truly gifted amateur chef, Robert N. Russell of New York. The three Russell brothers have a north woods hunting camp located on an isolated lake, where deer, grouse and water-fowl are abundant. Many years ago I was fortunate enough to be invited there for a week of deer hunting, and Weston, the senior brother, offered to "fly me up" in his float plane. After pointing out that Bob and Alex, his younger brothers, had preceded us to open the camp, he warned me to expect only the simplest food and accommodations.

Shortly after my arrival I should have recognized that my leg was being pulled to an amazing degree, for my comfortable birch-paneled room, adjoining bath, and the deep, comfortable chairs around the big hearth could hardly be termed "simple".

Dinner that night began with a fresh lobster cocktail, a grouse

---

*Today duck presses will cost upwards of three hundred dollars. They can be purchased at Bridge and Company in New York City.

consommé, and, finally, pressed duck. Hunger is reputed to be a fine sauce, but it did not compare with the sauce prepared by Bob for the four black ducks.

Before giving the recipe itself, let me put in a short warning on the *pre*-preparation of the ducks themselves. Too many amateurs follow the practice of wet-picking ducks, then soaking them for one hour or ten in salt water. The theory behind this barbaric practice is that the soaking "draws out the game flavor." If you want to eliminate this flavor, why not use domestic ducks in the first place? But not for pressed duck. The salt water immersion draws the blood from the duck, which is the last thing to be desired in the proper preparation of pressed duck. The juice makes the dish!

HOW TO COOK

After rubbing the ducks inside and out with salt and black pepper, place them *as is* in an oven preheated to 425 degrees for *exactly* twelve minutes. Remove from the oven, remove the skin from the breasts, then slice the meat from the breast in slices a quarter-inch thick, then put the meat to one side. The four carcasses are then placed in the press and the juices extracted. Melt two ounces of butter in the large chafing dish, stir in two tablespoons of black currant jelly, four tablespoons of Worcestershire sauce, four drops of Tabasco sauce, and the essence from the duck press. Stir until merged, then add the slices of duck breast. Place a cover on the chafing dish and let it simmer for five minutes. In the other chafing dish place two ounces of butter and the diced livers of the ducks, and when these are slightly browned, add four minced shallots, one minced carrot, one tablespoon of chopped parsley, ¼ teaspoon of marjoram, salt and pepper, four ounces of dry sherry, and simmer for ten minutes. Strain this and add to the sliced breasts and sauce in the large chafing dish, merging the two sauces thoroughly. Continue to simmer this for five minutes, with the cover removed from the chafing dish. Serve on warmed plates. With this, wild rice is a fine accompaniment, along with julienne string beans and a tossed lettuce salad with tart dressing. A slightly chilled rosé wine is fine to wash it down.

Requirements

4 mallards
   (black duck,
     canvasback or pintail)
⅛ pound of butter
¼ teaspoon marjoram
1 tablespoon of chopped
   parsley
4 shallots or four small
   white onions
2 tablespoons of black
   currant jelly
4 tablespoons of
   Worcestershire sauce
4 ounces of dry sherry
4 drops of Tabasco sauce
1 carrot
salt
freshly ground
   black pepper

Currituck Duck

Requirements

2 ducks (canvasback,
    mallard, pintail,
    black duck)
2 small onions
1 wineglass of dry sherry
⅛ pound of butter
2 bay leaves
½ teaspoon of marjoram
1 tablespoon of currant
    jelly
1 wineglass of dry red wine
salt
freshly ground black
    pepper
1 cup of chicken stock or
    chicken consommé

Bill Sharpe, a tarheel publicist of some renown, the creator of that culinary mystery known as "Frizzle-froed Chicken," has gone on more hunting expeditions without so much as pulling a trigger than any man in North Carolina or points south. While he has never been known to provide game, he is extremely capable at both preparing and eating it. Despite the fact that there have been numerous occasions when I was tempted to initiate action against him for libel and/or slander, I must give the d____ (Bill Sharpe, that is) his due when it comes to the preparation of Currituck duck. How he is on waterfowl from other portions of his beloved state, such as Pamlico, Roanoke or Albermarle Sounds, I do not know. But I can recommend his Currituck Duck, with or without the Yaupon Tea which Sharpe now imbibes in preference to the Essence of Cataloochie Corn which he once considered an integral part of the consumption of duck. For those who are interested in learning about Frizzle-froed Chicken, I can recommend a small but diverting volume entitled *Tar on My Heels,* written, edited and publi-*cized* by one William Sharpe.

HOW TO COOK

Rub ducks with salt and pepper and place in an oven preheated to 400 degrees for twenty-five minutes. Slice all the meat from the ducks and place in a warming oven. With a heavy knife or cleaver, chop the carcass of each duck in a dozen pieces and place in a large saucepan with ⅛ pound of butter, two small onions minced fine, 1 wineglass of sherry, 2 bay leaves, ½ teaspoon of marjoram, 1 wineglass red wine (dry), 1 tablespoon of currant jelly, salt and pepper, 1 cup of chicken stock. Boil until the liquid has been reduced to at least half, strain through a fine mesh strainer and serve as a gravy for the sliced duck. With this Sharpe (but not Camp) likes collard greens, grits, corn pone, and (recently) several cups of yaupon tea. Personally, I prefer it with green beans, grits, cornbread and a glass or two of claret.

It has been my good fortune to cross spoons with a number of fine cooks, professional and amateur, but few of them are in the class of Dr. Albert Simard of New York, Paris, and the Dungarvon. A French chef of the *bleu* would classify him as a "gifted amateur," for to Albert the preparation of food is a demanding art. He is an active member of several gourmet groups, and so far as I know is the only individual who has ever forcefully excluded my wife from her own kitchen. My own efforts in this direction have been unsuccessful. I was tempted to include some game fish recipes in this volume, if only to pass on Albert's favorite methods of preparing salmon and brook trout. However, I am indebted to him for the privilege of tasting and purloining some of his game recipes.

Many years ago he visited me for a weekend of duck shooting. I spent a large part of the day prior to his arrival in the preparation of a dish I knew he favored, Cassoulet Rhetoret. It was late December, and cold, and I had visions of rowing him out to my small cruiser at noon and surprising him with an earthenware pot full of piping-hot Cassoulet. It *was* cold, the wind blew a half gale and the ducks were flying. To my annoyance and irritation he flatly refused to leave the blind for lunch. "One can always eat later," he insisted, "but when will the birds fly like this?" He atoned for this on Sunday by preparing Caneton Simard.

HOW TO COOK

Blend one ounce of cognac with one ounce of Cointreau and rub the ducks thoroughly, inside and out, with this liquid. Place ⅛ pound of butter in a mixing bowl and when sufficiently soft work in 1 tablespoon of minced parsley, 1 tablespoon of dry basil, ½ cup of goose *pâté*, two minced shallots, ½ teaspoon of powdered ginger. When this is well blended merge with 1½ cups cooked rice. Stuff the ducks with this mixture. Place the ducks in a shallow roasting pan. In a separate saucepan, over a low flame, blend ⅛ pound of butter, the remainder of the cognac and Cointreau, 1 cup of orange juice, two tablespoons of lemon juice, and two cups of white wine. Pour this over the ducks and place them in an oven that has been preheated to 400 degrees. Baste frequently until the ducks are browned and tender. Remove the ducks to a warming oven. Place the roasting pan with the remaining juices over a low flame on top of the stove and stir and "scrape" until it is reduced to a thick gravy. Place ducks on a serving platter and pour gravy over them. With this Albert prefers julienne string beans, hearts of lettuce with a sharp dressing, and a chilled white wine as "dry as dry." I agree on *every* count.

Caneton Simard

Requirements

2 mallards (black duck, scaup, widgeon or pintail)
2 shallots
1½ cups of cooked rice
1 cup of orange juice
½ cup goose or chicken liver *pâté*
¼ pound of butter
1 tablespoon of chopped parsley
1 tablespoon dry basil
1 ounce cognac
1 ounce Cointreau
2 tablespoons of lemon juice
½ teaspoon of powdered ginger
2 cups of dry white wine

Cacciatore Garigliano

Requirements

3 mallards *(all waterfowl were "mallarda" to the Italian peasant)*
1 carrot
3 large *red* onions
1 large apple
3 ripe tomatoes
½ teaspoon oregano
½ teaspoon powdered saffron
4 cloves of garlic
2 cups of dry red wine
1 cup of dry white wine
⅔ cup of olive oil
salt
freshly ground black pepper

This recipe, one dear to my heart for many reasons, was the discovery but not the creation of one Colonel George L. King (now U.S.A. Ret.) who possessed many conflicting gifts. He was an outstanding professional soldier, an accomplished musician, possessor of an amazing fund of practical and fantastic information, and a dedicated amateur chef. He came up with this recipe after we had stolen a day with a shotgun on the Gaeta Marshes during the course of our slow, unsteady progress up the rough boot of Italy during World War II. Despite a woeful lack of culinary apparatus, George managed to *brew* this fragrant dish under extremely difficult conditions. The various ingredients were assembled with great effort, much pantomime, and through the aid of an Italian-English dictionary. In this Herculean task George received the dubious assistance of Lt. Col. Donald Kellet, who had what he considered an efficient, foolproof method of transposing English into Italian, which merely called for the addition of an "i," "a" or "o" to the English word. As he was a master of the gesture, his success often proved a suprise to all concerned. Our initial repast, needless to say, did not include the side dishes of green noodles, or hot, buttered French bread, but we had plenty of heavy red wine.

HOW TO COOK

Quarter the three ducks, rub with salt and pepper, and sauté slowly in a large earthenware (glazed) pot in ⅔ cup of olive oil. When the ducks are lightly browned, remove and put to one side. To the remaining olive oil in the pot add one diced carrot, three diced red onions, one peeled, cored and diced apple, three diced tomatoes, four minced cloves of garlic, ½ teaspoon of oregano, ½ "pinch" of powdered saffron, two cups of dry red wine, one cup of dry white wine, salt, pepper. When this has begun to simmer, return the ducks, place the lid on the pot, and simmer *slowly* for three hours. The aroma that will come seeping from the rim of the cover will make it extremely difficult to last out the three hours, but temptation must be conquered. With this Colonel King provided some black but delicious Italian bread and a tossed salad drenched in his "dressing *militaire*." We dipped the bread in the gravy and washed everything down with a very full-bodied Chianti. It was a truly memorable meal.

The "coot," in this instance, is not a coot, but a scoter, or, if you want to be truly technical, a *Melanitta Perspicillata*. Along with two close cousins, it is known as coot in the coastal waters of the Atlantic from Maine to Long Island. It is, undoubtedly, the most maligned game bird in the United States, both from the sporting viewpoint and as a table delicacy. Improperly prepared it has a consistency and flavor that could be compared with a section of old rubber tire that has been stewed with rotten herring. Properly prepared, it can be favorably compared with a ragout of which tenderloin of venison forms the prime ingredient — although I can conceive of no one using tenderloin of venison in a stew, even if you call it a ragout.

The late Luis Henderson was not a Cape-Codder, but he frequented that area, and he inevitably returned with new and succulent recipes for assorted chowders and stews. This one, he admitted, included a few personal touches that improved the interest as well as the flavor.

HOW TO COOK

Remove all of the fatty tissue (*all* of it) from the coot breasts, place them in a small crockery bowl and cover them with a marinade of the following — two medium onions sliced thin, two minced cloves of garlic, two bay leaves, three cloves, 1 tablespoon of cider vinegar, salt and pepper. Place them in the refrigerator and allow them to marinate for ten to twelve hours. When ready, cut ¼ pound of salt pork into quarter-inch cubes, place in a pot, and render the fat from the pork, removing the cubes when browned and place them to one side. Remove the breasts from the marinade and dry them thoroughly, then lightly brown them in the salt pork fat. Drain off the fat, and add the marinade along with 1 diced tomato, ½ teaspoon of tarragon, and the crisp cubes of salt pork. Place a lid on the pot and simmer slowly for two hours.

Barnstable Coot Stew

Requirements

breasts of three "coots"
2 medium onions
2 cloves of garlic
2 bay leaves
3 cloves
½ teaspoon of tarragon
¼ pound of salt pork
1 tomato
salt
freshly ground black
    pepper
1 tablespoon of cider
    vinegar

Scoter Brochette

Requirements

6 coot breasts
3 red onions
2 cloves of garlic
½ cup of wine vinegar
2 cups of dry red wine
2 tablespoons of lemon
    juice
4 tomatoes
½ teaspoon curry powder
6 slices of fat bacon
½ cup of olive oil
salt and pepper

Bob Russell, who insists that he works "out of Boston," never boils, fries, sautés, stews or simmers any form of meat if facilities are available to broil it, and to him charcoal is the only suitable medium for broiling. While many will agree as to his preference for charcoal, not every cook has these facilities at hand under all conditions. The inclusion of charcoal broiling units in many modern kitchens has done much to improve culinary satisfaction, but there are few recipes in which the gas or electric broiler cannot be substituted in a pinch.

Many years ago Russell, a stout defender of the lowly coot, who built a charcoal broiler in the kitchen of his shooting shack before he built the structure itself, proved quite conclusively that breast of "coot" or scoter, was fare deserving the praise of a gourmet. The small island on the coast of Maine where his shooting shack is located provides an abundance of coot, and since the limit on other waterfowl is low, Bob and his guests devote a certain amount of time to the pursuit of this humble bird.

HOW TO COOK

Remove *all* the fatty tissue from the breasts, and cut each breast — across the grain — into four pieces. Place to one side. In a saucepan place the following: one onion, minced fine, two minced cloves of garlic, ½ cup of wine vinegar, 2 cups of dry red wine, 2 tablespoons of lemon juice, ½ teaspoon of curry powder. Bring this to a boil, then simmer slowly for five minutes. Remove from the fire and allow it to cool. When cooled, place in refrigerator until cold. Place the sections of coot breast in a clay or china casserole and pour the chilled marinade over them, replace in the refrigerator and allow to marinate four or five hours. Remove coot sections from marinade and have four long broiling skewers at hand. On these skewers place one section of coot, a square of bacon, a slice of tomato, a slice of onion, square of bacon, section of coot, etc., etc. When each skewer has been "built up," place the ½ cup of olive oil in a flat pan, salt and pepper the meat and vegetables to taste, then rotate the skewers in the olive oil until the meat and vegetables have a film of this oil. Broil over a charcoal grill, turning skewers frequently, until meat is done.

This is another of Bob Russell's specialties, although he serves it "at home" rather than at the shooting shack, and many guests at his buffet suppers have admitted their defeat when it came to guessing the meat employed. So far as I know, Bob has never parted with the secret, but this lets the coot out of the bag.

HOW TO COOK

In a large skillet, melt ⅙ pound of butter. Slice 1 clove of garlic into four sections and brown this in the butter. Remove the garlic and sauté the coot breast which has been sliced *across the grain* in half-inch slices. Sauté until lightly browned and tender. Remove slices to warming oven. To the butter remaining in the skillet add 2 minced shallots, allowing them to brown slightly, then add ½ cup chicken stock, stir thoroughly over light flame, then add ½ teaspoon of basil and ¼ teaspoon of dried ground dill and 2 cups of sliced mushrooms. Simmer over very low flame for five minutes, then add ½ wineglass of sherry, salt and pepper to taste, then add slices of coot breast. Simmer over low flame for two minutes, then stir in 1 cup of sour cream that has been slightly warmed. It *does* resemble venison tenderloin.

Breast of Coot à La Russe

Requirements
4 coot breasts
2 shallots (or small white onions)
⅙ pound of butter
1 cup of sour cream
1 clove of garlic
½ teaspoon of basil
½ teaspoon of ground dill
2 cups of sliced mushrooms
½ cup chicken stock (or same amount chicken bouillon)
salt
freshly ground black pepper
½ wineglass of dry sherry

Stewed Duck Iliamna

Requirements

4 ducks (mallard,
    canvasback, pintail,
    scaup, widgeon)
1 cup of olive oil
12 small white onions
6 large carrots
2 cloves of garlic
2 cups of peas
    (fresh or canned)
1 pint of dry white wine
4 medium potatoes
salt
black pepper
½ cup of flour

Ray Peterson and Johnny Walatka, who range over most of Alaska in assorted aircraft, have a "joint" method of preparing duck that is rather simple, extremely filling, and very tasty. One insists that it is a Swedish method, the other that it is Polish, but as they always prepare it at Walatka's cabin on the bleak shore of Lake Iliamna, they compromise and call it "Stewed Duck Iliamna." As both of these characters enjoy good food, and have a wonderful time preparing it, the cabin is well stocked with what Peterson terms "herbs and simples." Although there were only three of us at the cabin, four ducks were prepared, with the explanation that Walatka works hard and therefore requires more nourishment than a lazy Swede and an itinerant writer. Peterson, incidentally, has the distinction of brewing the foulest coffee I have ever tasted, even in England.

HOW TO COOK

Quarter each of the ducks, rub with salt and pepper, dust with flour, and sauté until light brown in a large skillet with one cup of olive oil. Remove from skillet and put to one side. In a large earthenware casserole with a tight lid, place 12 small onions, 6 carrots (cleaned and cut in quarters lengthwise), two cloves of garlic minced, 2 cups of peas, four medium potatoes cut in quarters, salt and pepper to taste. Place the sautéed duck sections on top, add half the olive oil remaining in the skillet, one pint of dry white wine, place the cover on the casserole, and cook for two hours in a 300-degree oven. All in all, one thing blends with another, and the result is excellent. As lettuce was surprisingly scarce on Lake Iliamna, we had coleslaw, hot bisquits, and some old, leftover, dry white wine that Walatka had hidden under his bunk.

Charles Smith, who answers only to the name of "Smitty," will never receive the *cordon bleu,* because no one could persuade him to leave Andros Island for a longer period than it takes to go to Nassau and back. During the "off season" Smitty is the grand panjandrum of the kitchen at the Lighthouse Club at Andros Town, and it has been whispered that his talents are not exceeded by the bevy of French chefs who usurp him during the "on season." Smitty is one of the few persons I have ever encountered who might be termed a born cook. Whether he is preparing food for four or forty, he gives complete attention to every minute detail. His Bahamas Duck is a local recipe with Smith additions.

HOW TO COOK

Wipe the two ducks until dry and rub with salt and pepper, inside and out. Place in a roasting pan and put in an oven preheated to 400 degrees. Cook for 25 minutes, remove, and slice the meat from the ducks, then cut in bite-size pieces and put to one side. In a five-or six-quart pot put two tablespoons of butter and place over moderate flame until the butter is hot, then add one chopped tomato, two medium onions chopped fine, one clove of garlic (minced), and sauté for about three minutes, then add one diced carrot, the chopped carcasses of the two ducks, one bunch of celery cut in one-inch sections (including the leaves), one bay leaf, and four cups of water. Place the lid on the pot and cook over a brisk flame until the liquor has been reduced by half. Strain off this stock and return it to the pot, bring to a boil, and stir in 1½ cups of long-grain rice (first wash rice thoroughly and rinse it well), reduce the flame to a near minimum and cover the pot. After 25 minutes, add the pieces of duck and one teaspoon of paprika, salt and pepper to taste, stir slowly and carefully, and replace cover for ten minutes. Smitty serves this with fried plantain, pigeon peas and sliced avocado dipped in lime juice. It is enough to make a Bahamas beachcomber out of almost anyone. A conch chowder is usually the preamble to this, and it prepares the taste buds for the treat to come.

Bahamas Duck

Requirements
2 large ducks (mallard,
     black duck, pintail)
2 medium onions
1 bay leaf
1 clove of garlic
1 bunch of celery (small)
1½ cups of long-grain rice
2 tablespoons of butter
1 medium-size tomato
1 teaspoon of paprika
1 carrot
salt
freshly ground
     black pepper

Duck Grecco

Requirements

3 cups of boiled duck
  meat (bite size)
2 small onions
2 tablespoons of chopped
  parsley
1 bay leaf
1 teaspoon tarragon
1 clove of garlic
1 carrot
1 cup of sour cream
2 cups of chicken stock
  or consommé
1 wineglass of dry sherry
1½ cups of large green
  olives, pits removed
salt
freshly ground
  black pepper

Several years ago Ross Burkett, who has an isolated but comfortable hunting camp in Montana, twisted my arm to the point of no resistance in the matter of a big game hunt in his favorite wild but not woolly part of that state. On the afternoon of my arrival he called the two men who were to accompany us and suggested they drop in at his house after dinner to complete the plans for the expedition.

"We'll be two or three hours working out food, equipment and details," he glanced at Madame Burkett, "so I suppose we ought to have a snack when we're through."

The Madame nodded. "I've a couple of boiled ducks in the refrigerator," she admitted. "I can work something up with them."

Apparently she noticed that I winced slightly at the mention of "boiled" ducks, but she merely smiled sweetly and dropped the subject. That night, shortly before midnight, she served what I subsequently discovered to be Duck Grecco, and after my wince it took considerable prying to get the recipe.

HOW TO COOK

With the meat removed from the ducks the carcasses were cut up and placed in a large pot with 2 diced onions, 1 bay leaf, 1 teaspoon of tarragon, 1 minced clove of garlic, 1 diced carrot, two cups of chicken stock, and salt and pepper to taste. The mixture was brought to a boil, then the flame reduced to a simmer and the lid placed on the pot. This was simmered for two hours, and the stock strained into a smaller saucepan. The duck meat, 2 tablespoons of chopped parsley, 1 wineglass of dry sherry, and 1½ cups of large green olives (pits removed and each olive sliced into four sections) was added. This was allowed to simmer for another half hour until approximately one cup of stock remained, when 1 cup of sour cream was added. This was served on squares of toast, and there was not a complaint, although I did get an inquiring look from the cook. The term Grecco, I learned, was derived solely through the use of olives. Just as though there were no olives in Italy, Albania, Morocco and California. You can change the name. Still, it is excellent. I tried it later with some leftover goose, and it was just as good.

This method of preparing ducks came from a small inn near Carcassonne, in southern France, where it is served once each week as a specialty of the house. As I recall, it was on Wednesdays, and only during the fall. It took some figuring to work the ingredients down to the level of two ducks, but was finally accomplished, and tested on the spot with typical Gallic anxiety and thoroughness. Wednesdays are very popular nights at the Trois Soeurs.

HOW TO COOK

Quarter two ducks and place the sections in an earthenware pot. Salt and pepper to taste, then add 4 ounces of cognac, 1 cup of dry red wine, two large onions diced fine, 1 tablespoon of chopped parsley, ½ teaspoon of marjoram, ½ teaspoon of tarragon, 1 bay leaf, 1 minced clove of garlic, and four cloves. Stir slightly until this marinade is blended, then place a lid on the pot and allow it to stand in the kitchen (*not* in refrigerator) for six hours. At this time remove the duck sections. In a large skillet place ½ cup of olive oil and two tablespoons of butter. When hot, add the duck sections and brown well on both sides. Meanwhile, place the marinade over a low flame until it begins to simmer. Add the browned duck sections and ½ pound of sliced button mushrooms. Replace the cover on the pot and simmer for 1½ to 2 hours. At the Trois Soeurs the portions are served in small (not so small) individual casseroles. Several tiny boiled potatoes are placed around the rim of this casserole, and the duck and sauce is then placed inside. It is truly a rewarding dish. Especially with a dry claret.

Caneton au Vin

Requirements

2 mallards (black duck, pintail, canvasback, widgeon)
2 large onions
½ cup of olive oil
2 tablespoons butter
1 tablespoon of chopped parsley
4 ounces of cognac
1 cup of dry red wine
½ pound of button mushrooms
½ teaspoon of marjoram
½ teaspoon of tarragon
1 bay leaf
1 clove of garlic
4 cloves
salt and pepper

Duck Soup

This is one of my own recipes for duck soup. There are people who consider the term "duck soup" to be merely an ancient expression, but I like duck prepared in almost any form, and as there is almost always a lot of meat left on a duck carcass, it begs to be converted into soup.

Requirements

3 duck carcasses from
    which breasts have
    been consumed
½ cup of diced tomatoes
2 stalks of celery
3 medium-sized onions
1 large carrot
¼ teaspoon of tarragon
½ teaspoon of grated
    lemon peel
1 garlic clove
1 can of chicken consommé
½ cup diced cabbage
2 sprigs of parsley
2 quarts of water
salt
freshly ground
    black pepper

HOW TO COOK

In a large kettle place 3 duck carcasses cut in quarters, ½ cup of diced tomatoes, 2 stalks of celery, 3 medium-sized onions diced, 1 large carrot diced, ¼ teaspoon of tarragon, ½ teaspoon of grated lemon peel, 1 minced clove of garlic, ½ cup of chopped cabbage, 2 sprigs of parsley, 1 can of chicken consommé and 2 quarts of water. Add salt and pepper to taste. Bring to a boil, then reduce to a simmer, place lid on the kettle and simmer for 45 minutes. Remove the duck carcasses and carve off the meat, placing it to one side. Return the carcasses to the kettle, replace the lid, and simmer for 1½ hours. Strain through cheesecloth, skim off fat, and place the stock in a smaller kettle. Cut the duck meat into half-inch cubes, add to the soup stock, bring to a boil, pour into soup tureen and serve.

Spitted Duck

Requirements

2 black ducks
    (mallards, pintails,
    canvasbacks)
⅙ pound of butter
1 cup of red wine
1½ cups white wine
1 teaspoon rosemary
1 clove of garlic
¼ teaspoon tarragon
1 tablespoon chopped
    parsley
2 tablespoons Espagnol
    sauce

HOW TO COOK

Stuff two large ducks or four teal with any of the stuffings previously given. Melt ⅙ pound of butter in a saucepan and brown the hearts, livers and gizzards of the ducks, then add 1 cup of red wine and one cup of white wine, ½ teaspoon of salt, 1 teaspoon of rosemary, 1 minced garlic, ¼ teaspoon of tarragon, 1 tablespoon of chopped parsley. Place lid on the pan and simmer until stock is reduced to just under a cup. Use two or three stalks of celery tied together for a basting brush. Rub the birds with butter after they have been impaled on the spit, and place them three to four inches from the charcoal basket. Baste almost constantly with the wine-basting mixture. Chop the hearts, livers and gizzards and add them to the drip pan. When the birds are done, remove to a warming oven, place the drip pan over a medium flame, add ½ cup of white wine, and stir and scrape. Stir in two tablespoons of Espagnol sauce until gravy thickens, then serve separately.

When the big Canadian honkers arrive at the Outer Banks of North Carolina a goodly number of them rest a day or two and move in to Lake Mattamuskeet. The majority of the visitors to that area concentrate on hunting, to the exclusion of everything else, but a few knowing Yankees who like to crouch in a blind by day but sit at a bountiful board in the evening make certain of their reservation at Axton Smith's hostelry at Belhaven. For the old-timers Axton usually has a small private dinner before departure, and often these fortunates find that "Mom" has been pressed into service and persuaded to turn out roast goose. I learned, many years ago, that it is nice to come home with a large imposing gander, especially if you happen to have a friend you would like to impress by making him a present of the big bird. But for my own table, I hesitate when the echelon of big birds passes overhead, and pick out one of the goslings at the tail end of the "V". "Mom" also selects one of these more youthful, tender, if smaller birds for her Mattamuskeet Goose.

Mattamuskeet Goose

Requirements
1 eight-pound gosling,
    dry-picked
1 cup of mushrooms
½ pound chicken livers
1 pound of chestnuts
½ pound of sausage meat
6 ounces of Madeira
1 cup of chicken stock
    (or chicken bouillon)
½ teaspoon of rosemary
¼ teaspoon of dry
    tarragon
¼ pound fat salt pork
1 cup of dry white wine
1 cup of orange juice
2 tablespoons of lemon
    juice
salt
freshly ground black
    pepper
1 cup of heavy cream

HOW TO COOK

Place ½ pound chicken livers, goose liver and heart, 6 ounces of Madeira, 1 cup of chicken stock, ½ teaspoon of rosemary, ¼ teaspoon of dry tarragon in a saucepan and simmer under a cover until livers and heart are tender. Meanwhile, render fat from ½ pound of sausage meat, crumbling the meat in the pan while cooking. Score each chestnut on the flat face with a sharp knife and boil in salt water for 15 minutes. Allow to cool, then remove shell and skins and mash the meat with a fork. When chicken and goose livers are tender, remove from the pan and chop them fine. Return to the Madeira sauce, also adding at the same time 1 cup of mushrooms (sliced), the crumbled sausage meat and the chestnuts. Add salt and pepper to taste, and if the mixture is too moist add breadcrumbs until proper consistency is obtained. Slice fat salt pork into ¼ inch slices, then cut six strips, ¼ inch in diameter, from some of the slices. With larding needle, run three strips of salt pork (front to rear) down each breast of the goose, about ½ inch under the skin. Stuff the goose, after rubbing it inside and out with salt and pepper, place in a roasting pan, and place remaining strips of salt pork across the breast. Place in an oven preheated to 475 degrees for ten minutes. Meanwhile prepare a basting sauce by placing 1 cup of dry white wine, 1 cup of orange juice and 2 tablespoons of lemon juice in a saucepan and simmering for five minutes. Baste goose frequently until tender. When done remove to a warming oven, drain excess grease from roasting pan, add half cup of water and scrape pan while heating over light flame. Slowly add one cup of heavy cream to this gravy and serve with goose.

Cassoulet
St. Pierre

On the reedy margin of Lac St. Pierre, which is not a lake at all but a bulge of the St. Lawrence, is a small inn that, twenty years ago, was the September rendezvous for several American wildfowlers who made an annual pilgrimage for the early teal shooting. Madame Landre's small inn could accommodate only a half-dozen guests, but none of us ever considered staying at one of the larger, more elaborate hostelries. The beds were comfortable, the rooms spotless, and the food — *incomparable*. During the day we crouched in blinds or paddled the winding watercourses that cut the marshy island on the northern fringe of the lake. Few of us could wait until noon to open the large wicker hamper that was handed to each guest as he left the inn, long before first light. There was always enough, with some left over, for the shooter and his guide. The guide, inevitably, was one of the Adam brothers (pronounced Ah-damn), all of whom were hearty, if not discriminating, trenchermen. During the afternoon we speculated as to what Madame would give us for dinner. That was the quality of the cuisine.

It was here I tasted Cassoulet for the first time. I have eaten it scores of times since, in Paris, in the Midi, and in some of the better French restaurants in Quebec and the States. One of the smartest things I ever did was to persuade Madame Landre to *show* me the step-by-step preparation. My own Cassoulet has never approached that of Madame Landre, but I must confess that this dish as prepared by Charles Rhetoret (of Brodheads Creek fame) was a close second.

If you are pushed for time forget Casssoulet. It is a dish that calls for a certain amount of time and effort, and attention, but the results are rewarding.

HOW TO COOK

First, soak one quart of white navy beans for at least ten hours. Drain off the water and place the beans in a *large* earthenware casserole that has a tight lid. To the beans add 1 bay leaf, ¼ teaspoon rosemary, four large onions diced, 4 peppercorns, two cloves of garlic minced, ¼ pound of Italian salami diced in quarter-inch cubes, 1 cup of dry white wine, 2 teaspoons of chopped parsley, then cover with water. Place the lid on the casserole, put it in a 200- to 225-degree oven and let it go for six hours, checking occasionally to add water as needed. Two hours before time to serve, cut an eight-pound goose in eight to ten sections. Rub each section with salt and pepper. In a very large skillet put 4 ounces of olive oil. When the oil is hot enough to "explode" a drop of water tossed in it, add the sections of goose, and sauté until lightly browned. Reduce the flame and add two cups of dry white wine. Place a cover on the skillet and simmer briskly for thirty minutes. Remove the casserole from the oven and add the contents of the skillet, stirring the meat *carefully* into the beans. Replace the cover on the casserole and return to the oven at 250 degrees, for an hour and a half. Serve this with herb rolls (see back of the book) and a lettuce salad with a tart dressing, along with a bottle of well-chilled dry white wine. I can assure you of one thing — you will eat more than you should.

Requirements

1 eight-pound "wild" goose
¼ pound Italian salami
1 quart of white "navy" beans
1 bay leaf
¼ teaspoon rosemary
2 teaspoons chopped parsley
4 large onions
4 peppercorns
4 ounces of olive oil
2 cloves of garlic
3 cups of dry white wine
salt
freshly ground black pepper

Chesapeake Goose

Requirements

1 eight-pound Canada
    goose
1 quart (with liquor)
    medium-sized oysters
1 medium onion
2 cups of dry white wine
½ teaspoon of tarragon
½ teaspoon of rosemary
¼ pound of fat salt pork
5 drops of Tabasco sauce
⅛ pound of butter
¼ pound of chopped
    parsley
2 cups of soft breadcrumbs
½ teaspoon of paprika
1 cup of sour cream

In the cooking of a goose, the major differences seem to lie in the dressing (or stuffing). Although you might work up an interesting local argument on the matter, I have not found the honker from the Chesapeake to be more tender, succulent and flavorful than one from Mattamuskeet, Currituck, or Merrymeeting. If anything, I believe I would give a slight edge to a plump gosling that has been feeding for a month on the lush wild celery of Currituck. However, Bob Russell, who has provided several contributions to this volume, insists that "dressing *makes* the goose." Having partaken of his Chesapeake Goose, I must admit that I know of few epicures who would hesitate to give him a standing toast to his creation.

HOW TO COOK

In a saucepan place ⅛ pound of butter. When melted add 1 medium onion minced fine, sauté until onion is lightly browned, then add liver, heart and gizzard of goose that has been diced. Sauté until brown, then add 2 cups of dry white wine. Cover and simmer until liver, heart and gizzard are tender. In another saucepan place 1 cup of oyster liquor, ½ teaspoon of tarragon, ½ teaspoon of rosemary, 5 drops of Tabasco sauce, ¼ cup of chopped parsley, ½ teaspoon of paprika, and bring to a boil, stirring constantly. Reduce heat and simmer for five minutes. Place two cups of breadcrumbs in a large mixing bowl and pour this liquor over them. In another saucepan place the oysters with remaining liquor and simmer lightly for three minutes. Add to bowl with breadcrumbs, and carefully merge with a wooden spoon. This should be moist but not "soggy," so additional breadcrumbs may be needed. Care should be taken not to "break" the oysters. The salt pork should be now sliced into ¼-inch slices, and six ¼-inch diameter strips cut from some slices. With a larding needle, lard each breast with three strips of salt pork, ½ inch under the skin. Rub the goose inside and out with salt and pepper, stuff, place in roasting pan, and over the breast with the remaining slices of salt pork. Place in an oven that has been preheated to 475 degrees, then reduce to 400 degrees after ten minutes. Baste frequently with the sauce in which the liver, heart and gizzard were cooked. When the goose is tender, remove to a warming oven, skim grease from the roasting pan, and place pan over low flame. Add ½ cup of water and stir until thick gravy results, add liver, gizzard and heart, and one cup of sour cream. This gravy should be served on the slices of goose, but *not* on the stuffing. The stuffing is sufficient unto itself. If you doubt this, try it.

2

Grouse and Pheasant

OF ALL OUR game birds, these two undoubtedly are the favorites of those who prefer a *mild* rather than *firm* wild flavor. The gourmet has discovered that only through careful preparation can this flavor be preserved. Certain herbs, used in moderation, enhance rather than diminish this flavor, but the greatest loss in flavor results from overcooking. While this is true, in a greater or lesser degree, with almost all game birds (with the possible exception of the scoter), it is pronounced in the case of the grouse and pheasant. The former, by reason of its diet, normally has a more marked wild flavor than the pheasant, which is a farm-fringe rather than woodland creature.

With both these birds, it is preferable to use herbs in the "green" rather than dried form, but as these are not readily available in most areas, the majority of chefs, both amateur and professional, are forced to second best. Wherever possible, shallots should be used rather than onions, although some recipes definitely call for onions. For some reason, undoubtedly a sound one, many of the great chefs who take pride in their preparation of game flavor a "touch" of saffron in their game recipes. By a "touch" they mean just that, for this is one of the most penetrating herbs used in cookery. A "touch" too much and the only discernible flavor is of saffron.

In addition to careful preparation, both grouse and pheasant require frequent basting. In fact, it would be almost impossible to *over*-baste either of these birds. I have found the suction baster, which resembles a greatly oversize medicine dropper, to be the most practical and convenient method, for it is handy, effective, and does not require the oven door to be open as long as is normally necessary when the spoon is used. Two "squirts," fore and aft, and you have adequately basted the bird.

Overcook either grouse or pheasant and you have a dry, tough and flavorless bird. While the proper use of the modern aluminum foil is an aid to the lazy chef, it is not and never will be a substitute for proper basting. The broiled, roasted, or spitted bird should never be cooked until the meat "falls away from the bone." Only the bird cooked in stock or sauce should be cooked to this degree, for in such instances the juices are retained.

Properly prepared, both grouse and pheasant have a fine, delicate flavor, and the grouse ranks very high on the epicurean scale, probably second only to woodcock. But that is another chapter.

Howard "Ken" Belknapp has now reached the point where he is crowding fifty and has never found it vital, or desirable, to enter the marital state. One of the reasons for this may be that for the past twenty years he has been enjoying the culinary artistry of Howard, a Virginia Negro cook, who also serves as housekeeper, valet and general factotum. From his Chicago apartment it is not too much of a jaunt to his small but comfortable hunting and fishing camp, which Howard has stocked with every possible aid to fine cookery. Howard likes the camp better than the apartment, as it gives him more time to concentrate on cooking. Howard refuses to state where he found the recipe for Grouse Casserole Michigan, but he was willing to part with it.

HOW TO COOK

Disjoint two grouse and rub the sections with salt and pepper, then lightly dust with flour. In a large skillet melt ⅙ pound of butter and when hot add the grouse sections along with the diced livers, hearts and gizzards. Sauté until light brown, then remove. Line the bottom and sides of an earthenware casserole with paper-thin slices of Italian ham. Arrange the grouse sections in the bottom of the casserole. In the skillet, with the hearts, livers and gizzards, add four shallots diced fine, one clove of garlic minced, and sauté for two or three minutes. Then add one cup of dry white wine, 1 cup of button mushrooms, 1 tablespoon of minced parsley, ¼ teaspoon of basil, and a dash of Tabasco sauce. Bring to a boil and pour over the grouse in the casserole. Add another cup of dry white wine and place cover on the casserole. Cook for 1½ hours in a 350-degree oven. Stir in, carefully, one cup of sour cream, return to the oven for five minutes, then remove and serve.

Grouse Casserole Michigan

Requirements
2 grouse
⅙ pound of butter
1 clove of garlic
4 shallots
¼ teaspoon of basil
1 cup of button
    mushrooms
2 cups of dry white wine
½ cup of flour
1 dash of Tabasco sauce
1 tablespoon of minced
    parsley
¼ pound thinly sliced
    Italian ham
    (Prosciutto)
salt
freshly ground
    black pepper

Grouse Austin

Cash Austin, one of the really great northwoods wardens, was spoiled in his youth by lumber-camp cooking. In northern Maine the lumber-camp kitchen was lorded over by a French "chef" from across the line in Quebec, and few workers ever ate better than the lumberjack. The food was not only well prepared, but the preparation was varied. Having eaten of this, Cash vowed he was never going back to meat and beans and potatoes. When he had an opportunity he could prepare a really fine meal, even back in the woods, and I still find my taste buds are vibrating when I think of the dinner he prepared one evening on Togue Pond, 'way back of beyond.

We were going to be back in the bush for a week or ten days, and as my wife was along, Cash and the late Levi Dow, Warden Supervisor of Aroostook County for many years, had brought along a half-dozen live young chickens to add to the fare. These chickens, at camp, were tethered at intervals along a twenty-foot length of cord. Nancy, who could not "stomach" the idea of eating a chicken an hour or so after she had watched it cluck and pick, insisted that they be spared. As a matter of fact, we flew the chickens out with us, and the two "tough" wardens had become so attached to them that they exchanged them for six others — which they consumed with gusto. However, with the chickens ruled out, Cash decided that grouse would be a good substitute. It was.

The grouse were roasted in a reflector oven, and they provided the cleanest-picked bones I have ever seen.

HOW TO COOK

Melt ¼ pound of butter in a skillet, add the finely chopped hearts, liver and gizzards of the grouse, and sauté until browned and tender. Add two finely chopped small onions and four stalks of celery (leaves and all) finely chopped. Sauté for ten minutes over low heat, add ⅔ of a cup of water (or a similar amount of chicken stock or consommé if you have it). Bring to a boil and put aside to cool. Rub two grouse inside and out with salt and pepper. When onion-celery-liver, etc., is cool, add two cups of crumbled corn bread and stir until merged. Stuff the grouse with this; rub both birds with the remaining ⅛ pound of butter and place them in a shallow roasting pan in a 450-degree oven. After ten minutes reduce the heat to 350 degrees. Cook for one hour, basting *frequently*, or until tender. If necessary add a half-cup of hot water to the pan to aid in the basting. Blend the juice of one lemon and one jigger of dark rum. Pour this slowly over the birds, return to the oven for one minute, then remove and serve, pouring the pan juices over the birds when they have been placed on a hot platter. With this we had what Cash termed "blueberry bangbelly." He had brought along several jars of his wife's canned blueberries. One cup of strained blueberries was added to the cornbread mix, stirred in gently.

Requirements
2 grouse
2 small onions
¼ pound of butter
4 stalks of celery
2 cups of crumbled corn
    bread (Johnny cake)
1 lemon
1 jigger of dark rum
salt and pepper

Grouse Jaeger

Requirements

2 grouse
4 strips of fat bacon
1½ cups of cooked rice
4 shallots
⅛ pound of butter
6 ounces of Tokay or
    medium-dry
    sauterne (Graves)
⅔ cup finely shredded and
    chopped red cabbage
½ teaspoon of basil
¼ teaspoon of rosemary
½ cup of heavy cream
    (or sour cream)
salt
freshly ground
    black pepper

The grouse found in Austria are not the *Tympanuchus Cupido Americanus* but the *Perdix perdix,* or Hungarian partridge, and although smaller they have much in common with our ruffed grouse, at least in flavor. At Bluhnbach we had them served in several ways, but the finest, to my taste, was termed "Jaeger" or hunter style. This called for the use of Tokay wine, but I tried ruffed grouse prepared in the same manner, and unable to locate any Tokay at the time, I used a Graves sauterne, and it served admirably.

HOW TO COOK

Place ⅛ pound of butter in a skillet over a low flame. To this add 4 shallots minced fine, ⅔ cup of red cabbage, finely shredded then chopped, ½ teaspoon of basil, salt and pepper, and sauté for five minutes. Then add one ounce of medium-dry sauterne, stir, and add 1½ cups of cooked white rice, merging it thoroughly. Put to one side to cool. Rub two grouse inside and out with salt and pepper. Stuff the grouse with rice and place in a shallow roasting pan. Place two strips of fat bacon (lengthwise) across the breast of the grouse and pin in place with toothpicks. Place in an oven preheated to 450 degrees for 10 minutes. In a saucepan place 5 ounces of sauterne and ¼ teaspoon of rosemary. Bring to a boil, then remove from stove. Reduce flame in oven to 350 degrees and and baste grouse with rosemary-sauterne frequently (every 5 minutes). Continue to baste with drippings until grouse have been in the oven for one hour, or until tender. Remove grouse to platter and place in warming oven. Place roasting pan over low flame and add ½ cup of heavy cream very slowly, stirring and scraping pan constantly. Remove grouse from warming oven, pour the gravy over them and serve. Prepared in this manner the grouse lose none of their flavor, and the stuffing is delicious. (In my own preparation I added the liver, heart and giblets, chopped fine, to the skillet when I sautéed the cabbage and shallots, and included them in the stuffing.)

This was one of the favorite dishes at Bluhnbach, and as the cook had a Hungarian mother, it is not surprising that it was prepared with extreme care. In Hungary, paprika was included in just about everything but pancakes, according to several reliable sources.

Grouse Paprika Bluhnbach

HOW TO COOK

Cut three grouse lengthwise down the spine. In a skillet melt ⅛ pound of butter and slightly brown the grouse, removing them to an earthenware casserole when browned. In the skillet place 6 shallots diced fine, add ½ clove of minced garlic, and sauté over low flame for 5 minutes. Add ½ teaspoon of rosemary, ¼ teaspoon of tarragon, 3 ounces of dry sherry, 2 tablespoons of paprika, salt and pepper, 3 tablespoons of lemon juice and ½ cup of chicken stock. Bring to a boil, stirring constantly, then pour over the grouse in casserole. Place in an oven preheated to 400 degrees and cook for 45 minutes. Remove from oven, stir in 1 cup of sour cream, and return to oven for five minutes. Remove and serve. The meat does *not* fall from the bones, but it is tender and juicy, and *full* of flavor.

Requirements

3 grouse
6 shallots
3 ounces of dry sherry
2 tablespoons of paprika
⅛ pound of sweet butter
½ clove of garlic
½ teaspoon of rosemary
¼ teaspoon of tarragon
3 tablespoons of lemon
   juice
1 cup of sour cream
½ cup of chicken stock
   (or consommé)
salt
freshly ground
   black pepper

Grouse Brighton

Requirements

2 grouse
8 very small white onions
4 cloves
4 small carrots
¼ pound of chicken livers
2 tablespoons of chopped
    parsley
½ teaspoon of rosemary
1 pinch of powdered
    saffron
1 cup of breadcrumbs
2 eggs
⅛ pound of butter
½ cup of cream
1 quart of dry white wine
1 bay leaf
salt
freshly ground
    black pepper

This is another gem from the crown of Gene Brighton of Oregon, and while I am normally averse to "stewed" game, with very few exceptions, this happens to be one of the few. It has something in common with the *cocka-leekie* of Scotland, but with a touch of Gallic pressure. One of the big advantages of the dish, according to Gene, is that you can get it started, then get in two or three hours on the stream, and by the time it is ready you have a few trout for the first course. Even minus the initial course, it is a delightful dish.

HOW TO COOK

Melt ⅛ pound of butter in a small skillet, add ¼ pound of diced chicken livers, along with the diced livers, hearts and gizzards of the grouse, and sauté until browned. Soak 1 cup of breadcrumbs in ½ cup of cream. Turn contents of skillet, after cooling, into a mixing bowl and add creamed breadcrumbs, salt and pepper, then stir in two beaten eggs, ½ teaspoon of rosemary and 2 tablespoons of chopped parsley. Stuff the two grouse with this and sew the opening. Place the grouse in an earthenware casserole. Add one quart of dry white wine, 4 small carrots quartered lengthwise, eight small onions, one bay leaf, four cloves, salt and pepper, and one pinch of powdered saffron. Place lid on casserole and put in 300-degree oven for 2½ hours. I found that by adding three tablespoons of sauce Espagnol and ½ cup of sour cream to the stock in the casserole the gravy had added "body."

Oskar Lindstrom, whose grandfather emigrated from Sweden to Wisconsin seventy-five years ago, considers that he was unfortunate to be the only son of an only son, but there his misfortune ceased. He has a 600-acre farm that provides him with a very comfortable income, an abundance of game and more fish than he can use, plus four fine children, and a beautiful blond wife who is most certainly one of the finest cooks in the entire state. He also has two Brittany spaniels that are the envy of every birdshooter who hunts with him. The meals, *all* of them, *chez* Lindstrom, are memorable, but the dinners are exceptional, even considering the aquavit. Oskar explains that under *no* conditions should fish be eaten without the accompaniment of a glass of cold aquavit, and adds that in an emergency, "even pancakes can be considered fish."

HOW TO COOK

Quarter and dry three grouse. Rub them with salt, pepper and flour. Beat two eggs, with three tablespoons of water, and place 1 cup of dry breadcrumbs in shallow pan. Roll grouse quarters in egg, then in breadcrumbs, salt and pepper. In a large skillet melt ¼ pound of butter. Place one split clove of garlic in butter and brown, then remove. Sauté grouse quarters in butter slowly until browned. Remove grouse and place in a shallow earthenware casserole. Place in an oven preheated to 350 degrees and allow them to remain for 20 minutes. Add one cup of sour cream and sprinkle with ½ teaspoon of powdered dill (or two sprigs of fresh dill). Replace cover on casserole and return to oven for another 20 minutes. Add another cup of sour cream and return to oven for final 20 minutes. Remove and serve with gravy. The grouse is tender, and has lost none of its natural flavor.

Grouse Casserole

Requirements

3 grouse, quartered
½ cup of flour
1 cup of breadcrumbs
¼ pound of butter
1 clove of garlic
½ teaspoon of dill, powdered (or 2 sprigs of fresh dill)
2 eggs
2 cups of sour cream
salt
black pepper

Spitted Grouse (or Pheasant)

Requirements

3 grouse (or 2 pheasants)
½ pound of butter
1 lemon
2 cups of dry white wine
12 sprigs of parsley
1 small onion
1 teaspoon of tarragon
1 dash of Tabasco sauce
2 tablespoons
    Worcestershire sauce
salt
freshly ground
    black pepper

This is my favorite method of preparing either grouse or pheasant, but unfortunately it is within the reach of only those who happen to be in possession of a grill and spit. No other method, in my opinion, can produce a finished product as juicy, and tender and full of flavor. The spit and grill, because of the increased interest in this form of cookery, can be obtained at a very reasonable cost today, and should be an integral part of every household in which good cooking is considered important. I cannot even recall where I obtained the "requirements" for this recipe, but I have found it to be excellent (varying only in quantity) for all game birds, as well as chickens and turkeys. Anyway, here it is.

HOW TO COOK

Rub three grouse, inside and out, with salt and pepper. In a saucepan melt ¼ pound of butter and add 1 minced onion. When onion is browned, add 2 cups of dry white wine, 1 teaspoon of tarragon, 1 dash of Tabasco sauce, 2 tablespoons of Worcestershire sauce, salt and pepper. Place a cover on the saucepan and simmer slowly for fifteen minutes. Strain and add the juice of one lemon. With a small stick and string, make a brush of 12 sprigs of parsley. Place grouse on spit and baste liberally with the basting before putting on turnspit. Place drip pan under spit, and baste grouse frequently while turning, using brush of parsley and drippings when basting fluid is gone. Turn until golden brown and tender, and serve. This method seems to *seal* the flavor and juices in the birds. I prefer this served with baked macaroni and cheese, lima beans in cream, a lettuce salad with a very tart dressing, and a chilled bottle of Tavel. Herb rolls also would be included, as long as I'm wishing.

The late Jean Vallons, who operated a very small but fine hunting and fishing camp in Quebec, scoured that province until he located a fine chef, then proceeded to spend a good part of his own day in the kitchen. At no time did Jean have more than six sportsmen at his camp and, so far as I know, at no time did he have less than six. His prices were high, but the fishing was excellent, the hunting productive and the cuisine *superb*. Jean had a conviction that the French were the finest cooks in the world, but only when they adapted themselves to the offerings from other countries. He was eighty-two when he died, and during his lifetime he had sampled the cooking of the fine chefs from most of the western world. He had two favorite methods of preparing grouse, one quite simple, the other rather complex, but both were magnificent.

Grouse Royale

Requirements
3 grouse
¼ pound of butter
2 cups of oven browned breadcrumbs
½ cup of chicken stock
½ cup of chopped black walnuts
¼ cup of chopped blanched almonds
2 tablespoons of sugar (brown sugar preferred)
½ cup of black currants
1 cup of dry sherry
2 egg yolks
salt
freshly ground black pepper

HOW TO COOK

First, soak ½ cup of black currants in 1 cup of dry sherry for at least six hours. Then, in a saucepan, melt ⅛ pound of butter and stir in 2 cups of oven-browned breadcrumbs, ½ cup of chopped black walnuts, ¼ cup of blanched white almonds. Strain off sherry from currants and add currants to saucepan, placing sherry to one side. When dressing is cool add the yolk of two eggs which have been beaten with two tablespoons of brown sugar. Stir this into the dressing thoroughly. Rub three grouse inside and out with salt and pepper, then stuff with the dressing. Sew the openings. Rub the grouse with ⅛ pound of butter, patting the soft butter thickly on the breasts. Place in a shallow roasting pan in a oven preheated to 450 degrees for ten minutes. Reduce oven to 325 degrees, basting grouse *frequently* with the sherry in which currants were soaked, for additional hour. Remove grouse to hot platter and warming oven, and place roasting pan over low flame on stove, add ½ cup of water, stirring and scraping pan until gravy is formed. Pour over grouse and serve.

Grouse Vallons

This is the "simple" method of preparation, but no less tasty.

Requirements

3 grouse
¼ pound of butter
2 shallots
1 tablespoon of minced
    parsley
2 lemons
¼ pound of chicken livers
1 cup of white wine
¼ teaspoon of tarragon
1 pinch of thyme
salt
freshly ground
    black pepper

HOW TO COOK

In a small saucepan melt ⅛ pound of butter, add two shallots, minced, ¼ pound of chicken livers, and the livers, gizzards and hearts of the three grouse. Sauté for five minutes over low flame, then add 1 cup of dry white wine, 1 tablespoon of minced parsley, salt and pepper, ¼ teaspoon of tarragon, juice of 1½ lemons, one pinch of thyme, and simmer for ten minutes. Remove livers, gizzards and hearts and put through a meat grinder. To the ground livers, gizzards and hearts add the juice of half a lemon, mashing to a paste, then put to one side. Strain the stock for basting and put to one side. Split three grouse down the spine, rub with salt and pepper, then coat the skin side of the grouse with ⅛ pound of butter. Place grouse in very shallow pan, then place under a preheated broiler, about two inches from the flame. Baste frequently with wine-stock and drippings. Meanwhile, prepare six large pieces of toast, spread them with liver-gizzard-heart paste, and place them on a hot platter in warming oven. Broil until browned and tender, then remove grouse, placing each on a slice of toast. Place broiling pan on stove over light flame and add ½ cup of water, stirring and scraping pan until gravy forms. Pour this gravy over half-grouse on toast and serve.

Note:

Because of the variation in the heat of broilers, it is impossible to give the exact amount of time which the grouse should be broiled, but once the breasts are tender the birds should be removed immediately. Overcooking will ruin both the flavor and texture.

C.E. (June) Murray, co-founder and permanent vice-president of the Feather Duster Club, a very small and very exclusive shooting group from the metropolitan area of New York, enjoys shooting, cooking and eating pheasants. June, one of the finest sportsmen this recipe compiler has ever known, has very firm ideas on all three factors relating to the pheasant — namely, the shooting, cooking and eating. Many years ago the Feather Dusters did most of their pheasant shooting at June's large farm near Kingston, N.J., and enjoyed the hospitality at his rambling colonial farmhouse, from which every female member of the family had been banished. One of his favorite methods of preparing pheasant was rather simple, but it insured the retention of all the flavor and essence of the bird.

HOW TO COOK

Boil ½ pound of chestnuts for 15 minutes, allow to cool, then remove the meat. In a saucepan melt ⅛ pound of sweet butter, and in it brown 1 clove of garlic split in half. Remove garlic and add two shallots minced. Sauté for two minutes over light flame, then add the diced livers, hearts and gizzards of pheasants. Sauté for ten minutes over low flame, then add ½ cup of Madeira, 1 cup of sliced button mushrooms, ¼ teaspoon of rosemary, one pinch of thyme, salt and pepper; add crumbled chestnuts and stir thoroughly. Rub the two pheasants inside and out with salt and pepper, stuff with the chestnut dressing, and sew opening. Rub pheasants well with ⅛ pound of sweet butter. Rub two brown paper bags (8″ by 14″) with lard, place the pheasants inside the bags, tie the end of each bag with string, and place in a shallow roasting pan, then in an oven preheated to 400 degrees. After 10 minutes reduce the heat to 350 degrees and cook for 1 hour and 15 minutes. With a tart cranberry sauce, wild rice, braised celery, and a bottle of chilled Rhine wine, this will be a meal you will long remember.

Pheasant Murray

Requirements
2 pheasants
½ pound of chestnuts
1 cup of button
    mushrooms
¼ pound of sweet butter
2 tablespoons of lard
½ cup of Madeira
¼ teaspoon of rosemary
1 clove of garlic
2 shallots
1 pinch of thyme
2 large brown paper bags
salt
freshly ground
    black pepper

Pheasant Pierre

The Pierre in this instance is not the name of the French chef responsible for the method, but refers to Pierre, South Dakota, a state which today probably has a larger pheasant population than any other in the Union. A friend who prides himself on his culinary aptitude went to South Dakota several years ago, when a shooter could kill almost as many pheasants as he could carry, and returned with a freezer-load of birds and a recipe. He insisted it cost him a case of good bourbon to pry the recipe from a friend's cook, and he was equally insistent that it was well worth the cost. I tried it, and was almost willing to agree.

HOW TO COOK

Quarter two pheasants. In a paper bag place ¾ cup of flour, salt and pepper, and shake until mixed. Drop in quartered pheasants one piece at a time, shake bag and put floured sections to one side. In a large skillet heat one cup of olive oil. Drop in one split clove of garlic, and remove garlic when well browned. Brown the pheasant quarters well in the olive oil, remove and drain. In an earthenware casserole place four tablespoons of the olive oil in which the pheasant was browned, then arrange the pheasant sections in the casserole. Sprinkle with ¼ teaspoon of basil, add two shallots minced fine, 1 cup of button mushrooms, 1 tomato sliced thin (dip first in boiling water and remove skin from tomato), salt and pepper, then add one cup of dry white wine and one cup of dry red wine. Place cover on casserole and put in 350-degree oven for 1½ hours. Remove cover from casserole and return to the oven for another 20 minutes. Add one cup of sour cream, place cover back on casserole, and return to the oven for five minutes. Serve with brown rice, broccoli hollandaise, and hot garlic bread. A bottle of chilled rosé wine goes very well with this, although the man who "bought" the recipe insists a light claret is much better.

Requirements
2 pheasants
1 cup of olive oil
1 clove of garlic
¼ teaspoon of basil
1 cup of dry white wine
1 cup of dry red wine
2 shallots
1 large tomato
1 cup of button
    mushrooms
⅔ cup of flour
1 cup of sour cream
salt and pepper

This recipe has a strong flavor of Pennsylvania Dutch, which is not surprising in view of the fact that its donor, who prepared it for me, comes from a farmhouse not much more than a long musket shot from Lancaster. The farmhouse kitchen had an ancient coal range, but it lacked nothing in the way of spices and herbs, and was redolent of the secret ingredients that go to make up the inevitable seven sweets and seven sours. Food was prepared slowly and carefully, yet with complete ease.

Pheasant with Dumplings, Van Meer

HOW TO COOK

In a saucepan place one tablespoon of butter (from the ¼ pound) and over a moderate flame sauté one minced onion and half a stalk of celery diced fine. Soak one cup of breadcrumbs in a half-cup of heavy cream, place in a mixing bowl and stir in one cup of mashed sweet potato, ½ teaspoon of rosemary and the contents of the saucepan. Rub two pheasants inside and out with salt and pepper, then stuff with the dressing and sew opening carefully. In a large earthenware pot place 3 cups of chicken stock, ¼ teaspoon of powdered ginger, 3 stalks of celery, one cup of beer, two medium-sized onions minced fine; place cover on pot and bring to a boil, then remove cover, add the two stuffed pheasants, and reduce heat to a simmer. Allow to simmer for 2 hours. Meanwhile place remainder of ¼ pound of butter in a mixing bowl and work with a spoon until soft and creamy, work in three eggs, beating the mixture thoroughly after each egg is added. Beat in ½ teaspoon of salt, then add 1¼ cup of flour which has been blended with 1½ teaspoons of baking powder. Mix thoroughly, then shape into a long roll about 1 inch in diameter and allow to set for a least twenty minutes. When pheasants are tender (2 hours should be adequate) remove them to a serving casserole and place in a warming oven. Break off one-inch chunks of the dough and drop, one at a time, in the pheasant stock, which has been brought to a low boil. Remove the dumplings shortly after they rise to the top, and place in the casserole with the pheasants. Strain the stock, pour it on the pheasant and dumplings and serve. The pheasants should be carved at the table. With them Mrs. Van Meer served spiced stewed tomatoes, green beans, cabbage slaw with a sweet-sour dressing, and a wide assortment of traditional sweets and sours.

Requirements
2 pheasants
3 medium-sized onions
3 cups of chicken stock
¼ teaspoon of powdered ginger
½ teaspoon of rosemary
1 cup of mashed sweet potato
1 cup of breadcrumbs
½ cup of heavy cream
1 cup of beer (drink the rest of the bottle)
¼ pound of butter
3 eggs
1¼ cups of sifted flour
½ teaspoon of salt
1½ teaspoons of baking powder
3 stalks of celery

Pheasant Supreme

Requirements

2 large cock pheasants
2 cups of browned
    breadcrumbs
1 wineglass of cognac
½ pint of dry red wine
¼ pound of butter
1 ounce of Cointreau
2 tablespoons of grated
    orange peel
½ cup of orange juice
1 egg
4 stalks of celery
¼ teaspoon of chervil
1 pinch of basil
2 pinches of rosemary
salt
freshly ground
    black pepper

It is charged, and not without some reason, that the only good restaurants in England are those with imported chefs. When you pass by roast beef with Yorkshire pudding and mutton with caper sauce, you have touched the epitome of the English menu, but a friend with whom I spent a number of wonderful shooting holidays has a cook who is English to the core, yet can turn out dishes that would be the envy of many a chef on the warmer side of the Channel. Among the many really pleasant surpises was Pheasant Supreme, which the amateur chef can prepare when he wants to make a real impression on the visiting gourmet.

HOW TO COOK

Rub two fat cock pheasants with salt and pepper then coat the breasts with ⅛ pound of butter. In a saucepan heat up ⅛ pound of butter, and sauté 4 stalks of celery chopped fine (including leaves) for 5 minutes, mix in 2 cups of browned breadcrumbs, stir and blend for 2 minutes over low flame, then remove saucepan from fire and add 1 wineglass of cognac, 2 tablespoons of grated orange peel, ½ cup of orange juice, salt and pepper, one egg beaten well, ¼ teaspoon of chervil and one pinch of basil. In another saucepan steep 2 pinches of rosemary in one cup of dry red wine until faint steam rises from wine, then remove and stir in one ounce of Cointreau. Stuff the pheasants with the dressing, sew up openings, and place in shallow roasting pan in oven preheated to 450 degrees for 10 minutes. Reduce heat to 300 degrees and baste *frequently* with wine-rosemary-Cointreau basting, and when it is gone, baste with drippings. After 45 minutes in 300-degree oven, remove pheasants to platter and warming oven. Place roasting pan over low flame on stove, add ½ cup of warm water, stir and scrape until thick gravy results. Pour gravy over birds and serve. The pheasants will be neither overcooked nor undercooked, but crisp of skin, tender and juicy. Frequent basting is the secret. The orange flavor enhances and compliments rather than subdues the flavor of the pheasants.

This is a magnificent dish for those who would like to impress a few choice guests at a buffet, but it calls for a bit of careful timing at the end. It sprang from the Gourmet and Wine Club, mentioned in my Foreword — a group of which I had the pleasure to be a member many years ago. There were only fourteen members in the club, none of us in high financial brackets (quite the opposite), but all of us interested in cookery, wine and eating. We managed to assemble sufficient funds to rent a large room with a kitchen and bath in an elderly brownstone in Greenwich Village. Each week six members were assigned one course each, and lots were drawn for the responsible course. Everyone "chipped in" to provide the raw products and wine, and everyone assembled to taste and criticize. Several of the recipes in this volume were provided by members of this small, happy group. Recipes are scaled down to size.

HOW TO COOK

Quarter two pheasants. In a brown paper bag place ½ cup of flour, 1 teaspoon of salt, ¼ teaspoon of black pepper, and shake until merged. Place pheasant sections in bag and shake well until coated with flour. In a large skillet melt ⅙ pound of butter and in this brown one clove of garlic cut in half. Remove garlic when browned. Place sections of pheasant in skillet and brown well on both sides. Reduce flame to low simmer and add the following: 1 carrot chopped fine, four shallots minced fine, ¼ teaspoon of chervil, ¼ teaspoon of tarragon, 1 pinch of basil, 1 cup of button mushrooms sliced, 1 tablespoon of chopped parsley, ½ cup of dry white wine, 1 cup of chicken stock, salt and pepper to taste. Place a cover on the skillet and simmer slowly for 20 minutes. Remove cover and simmer for an additional 10 minutes or until pheasant is tender. Place pheasant and sauce in a chafing dish over an alcohol flame, and just before serving add one wineglass of cognac, then touch a match to the contents, which will flame beautifully for at least a quarter-minute. Serve with wild rice (by all means), hot garlic bread, and a tossed salad with lettuce, peeled and quartered tomatoes, avocado slices, and a tart dressing. You can't *miss* making an impression.

Pheasant Chasseur

Requirements
2 pheasants
⅙ pound of butter
1 wineglass of cognac
4 shallots
1 carrot
¼ teaspoon of chervil
¼ teaspoon of tarragon
1 pinch of basil
1 cup of button
    mushrooms
½ cup of dry white wine
½ cup of flour
1 tablespoon of chopped
    parsley
1 cup of chicken stock
    (or consommé)
salt
freshly ground black
    pepper
1 clove of garlic

Pheasant Peasant

This is another recipe garnered from the Gourmet and Wine Club, and is an original. It was successful to the point that it was a command performance at least three times each year. It can be prepared by the most amateur of chefs, provided he will follow the rules laid down for the course.

Requirements

2 pheasants
2 cups of browned
    breadcrumbs
½ cup of olive oil
¼ cup of lemon juice
1 cup of pitted ripe olives
1 shallot
1 clove of garlic
1 pinch of oregano
2 pinches of chervil
⅛ pound of butter
1 cup of dry red wine
2 stalks of celery
salt
freshly ground
    black pepper

HOW TO COOK

Rub two pheasants inside and out with salt and pepper. Prepare a stuffing as follows: in a saucepan melt ⅛ pound of butter, to this add two stalks of celery minced fine, one shallot minced fine, one clove of garlic minced fine. Sauté over low flame for five minutes. Add salt and pepper, 1 cup of sliced, pitted black olives, 1 pinch of oregano, 2 pinches of chervil and 2 cups of browned bread-crumbs. Moisten to proper consistency with liquor from olives. Stuff the pheasants with this dressing and sew openings. Place in a shallow roasting pan in an oven preheated to 450 degrees for ten minutes. Meanwhile, in a saucepan place one cup of dry white wine, ¼ cup of lemon juice and ½ cup of olive oil. Bring to a boil, then remove from the flame. Reduce the oven to 350 degrees and baste frequently with oil-lemon juice-wine until pheasants are tender. Approximately 45 minutes at 350 degrees. With this, the members agreed unanimously, the only wine to be sipped was a Lacrima Christi, which is produced in reasonable quantities by reliable vintners on the slopes of Mount Vesuvius. There are a few "brands" of this wine which, contrary to general opinion, will "travel." There are a few enthusiasts of the grape in Italy, however, who insist that it should not be touched at any point more distant than Naples or Amalfi.

So far as I know, no one has ever established definitely (other than through recourse to Government files) whether Peter Conraad is Swedish, Norwegian, or Danish. Speaking all three of these languages fluently, he describes himself as a "Scandahoovian." Peter does not, as some of his friends insist, "live to eat," but he freely admits that life without good food would not be worth living. The proper preparation of food, the careful evolution of a fine recipe, he insists, is an art that ranks with painting, sculpture and music. Peter refuses to eat "heavily or hurriedly." Many years ago he had a penthouse studio where he turned out fine miniatures. Although a member of the Gourmet and Wine Club, he disagreed violently with many members on the basis of the "quantity" of the food served. Occasionally he would invite a few of us to dinner, a ritual that occupied at least four hours, during which conversation ranged from fishing and shooting to literature and philosophy, this conversation guided by Peter as deftly as was the menu. A fine sherry, a few choice hors d'oeuvres, soup, fish, game, salad, and a small savory or cheese, special coffee and a rare brandy. When you were finished you were not logy or drowsy, for the portions were small but perfectly prepared and presented. Food was prepared in one corner of the large studio room, so the host carried on a conversation with his guests during its preparation. Here are two of his dishes, one of grouse, the other of pheasant.

Pheasant Conraad

Requirements
2 pheasants
⅔ cup of olive oil
3 cloves of garlic
1½ teaspoons of dried
    rosemary
¼ teaspoon of tarragon
⅔ cup of Marsala
1 tablespoon of lemon juice
½ cup of white wine
salt
freshly ground
    black pepper

HOW TO COOK

Cut two pheasants in serving portions and rub thoroughly with salt and freshly ground black pepper. In a large skillet place ⅔ cup of olive oil and three cloves of garlic split in quarters. Brown the garlic, remove it and throw it away. Brown the pheasant sections well in the olive oil over a moderate flame, sprinkle with 1½ teaspoons of dried rosemary (or 2 teaspoons of fresh chopped rosemary), ¼ teaspoon of dry tarragon (rubbed in the palms to a powder), add a touch more salt and freshly ground black pepper, ⅔ cups of Marsala, ½ cup of white wine (not too dry, Graves is excellent), the juice of half a lemon (or one tablespoonful), place a lid on the skillet and simmer very slowly for about 20 minutes, or until the meat is tender. If necessary, add a bit more white wine to keep the skillet from drying, and baste with the juice frequently.

Grouse Conraad

Requirements

2 grouse
½ cup of olive oil
1 cup of large green olives,
    pitted and quartered
2 cloves of garlic
1 cup of diced tomatoes
    (peeled if fresh,
    drained if canned)
1 cup of dry white wine
¼ teaspoon of thyme
1 pinch of tarragon
1 dash of Tabasco sauce
salt
freshly ground
    black pepper
½ cup of sour cream

HOW TO COOK

Split two grouse lengthwise, rub thoroughly with salt and pepper and dust lightly with flour. Place ½ cup of olive oil in a skillet and add two minced cloves of garlic, then the split grouse, browning them thoroughly and turning them frequently, but use only a moderate flame. Add 1 cup of diced tomatoes, 1 pinch of tarragon, ¼ teaspoon of thyme, 1 cup of dry white wine and 1 dash of Tabasco sauce. Stir well, place a cover on the skillet and simmer for 15 minutes, turning occasionally. Remove grouse to a hot plate and a warming oven, add one cup of pitted, quartered green olives and simmer for 5 minutes without the cover on the skillet. Add ½ cup of sour cream, stir and scrape until gravy thickens, pour over the birds and serve.

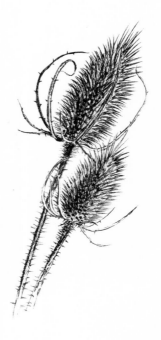

When the Feather Dusters Club met, this soup was a traditional meal-starter. Without it members have been known to sulk and seriously consider drafting a petition to depose the permanent vice president. Such petitions, of course, never gained names, for there was always the hope that the lapse would be remedied at the next meeting. "Besides," George Horn always pointed out, employing the Hungarian metaphor, "Murray owns the gun."

Pheasant Soup Murray

Requirements

1 plump cock pheasant
1 cup of button
    mushrooms
4 stalks of celery
1 grated carrot
4 leeks
2 sprigs of fresh dill
    (or ¼ teaspoon
    powdered dill)
1 teaspoon of rosemary
2 dashes of Tabasco sauce
2 half-inch-thick slices of
    white bread
½ teaspoon of grated
    lemon peel
⅛ pound of butter
¼ teaspoon of chervil
2 pinches of oregano
1 pinch of thyme
salt
pepper

HOW TO COOK

In a large pot place 1 large cock pheasant, 4 stalks of celery with the leaves, 1 grated carrot, 4 leeks, 2 sprigs of fresh dill, 1 teaspoon of rosemary, ½ teaspoon of grated lemon peel, 2½ quarts of water and 2 dashes of Tabasco sauce. Bring to a boil then reduce heat to a simmer, place a cover on the kettle, and simmer slowly for 1 hour. Remove the pheasant, peel off the skin and return to the kettle, carve the meat from the bird and put it to one side. Chop the carcass into several pieces and return to the kettle, replace the lid and simmer slowly for 1½ hours. Remove from fire, strain the stock through cheesecloth, skim off the fat, and place the resulting stock, now about 1½ quarts, into another kettle, add the meat carved from the pheasant cut in half-inch cubes, and one cup of thinly sliced button mushrooms and simmer for 5 minutes. Remove the crust from 2 half-inch-thick slices of bread and cut into half-inch cubes. In a small skillet place ⅛ pound of butter and stir in ¼ teaspoon of chervil, 2 pinches of oregano and one pinch of thyme. Add the cubes of bread and stir carefully over very low flame until cubes are coated with butter and herbs. Place the cubes in a large pie tin and put in a 300-degree oven until well browned. Add salt and pepper to taste to the soup and ladle out into warmed soup plates. Add eight or ten of the crisp croutons and serve.

3
Quail

A SMALL BIRD, but not without distinction. Anyone south of that invisible line drawn on the map by Messrs. Mason and Dixon will insist that this constitutes a miracle of understatement. The quail has distinction, not only as a game bird, but as a mouth-watering morsel for the gourmet. There are about four general offshoots of the quail family in the United States, and a few crosses, but there is only a slight difference in size and only local variations in the degree of flavor.

Difficult though the bird is to obtain — unless you do your own shooting — and requiring some effort to prepare and cook properly, the end is always rewarding. The French insist it is a "bird for sauces," but, in line with the old song — "It ain't necessarily so." The quail is a delectable dish with or without sauces, provided proper attention is given to preparation.

In the first place, despite the problems involved, it should be plucked and *not* skinned. Not that the skin has especially edible qualities, but merely that it prevents the bird from drying out during cooking. The bird has a definite flavor, and there are herbs that enhance it. It can be sautéed, broiled, stewed or roasted, but in all these methods the time element must be regarded, for the quail is a small bird and has little natural fat. According to my friend Colonel George L. King, a real expert on quail cookery, the bird should be cooked quickly and eaten immediately. No delays on quail.

Although few American sportsmen realize it, the quail is present in several parts of Europe as well as the southern portion of the States. It has suffered seriously in most of its range as a result of radical changes in agricultural practices during the past thirty years, and although the bird was found in fair numbers as far north as Connecticut, New Jersey now appears to be the northern margin. In Europe it is a prized bird of the gourmet, and can be bought on the open market — but in small quantities. Southern Italy has an excellent flight (yes, I said flight) in the spring and fall, when the birds move back and forth across the Mediterranean. An American quail couldn't fly two miles without touching down, yet the European bird makes nonstop flights of two hundred.

So much for the background of the bird, which was added merely in the hope of stimulating greater appreciation for it and to provide an incentive for careful preparation. Slowly, but quite surely, the bobwhite seems to be on its way out, so enjoy it while you can. Come the Revolution you'll eat coot — and like it!

In the preface to this chapter I mentioned Colonel George L. King, professional soldier and amateur cook, who, I believe, is inclined to pass off this recipe as one of his own variations. I am now in the position to contradict him, which was not always the case, so I must insist that this method of preparation stemmed from one Eugenio Gallo, a citizen but no longer a resident of Naples. Gallo not only took the Colonel and me on our first Italian quail shoot, which was extremely successful, but he prepared for us our first Italian quail.

HOW TO COOK

Drain the oil from eight small artichoke hearts and save the oil. In a saucepan place 1½ cups of dry white wine and the eight artichoke hearts. Bring to a boil and immediately remove from heat. Remove and cool the hearts of artichoke. Rub the inside of eight quail with salt and pepper, push one large pitted olive into the stomach cavity of each bird, follow this with an artichoke heart, and plug with browned breadcrumbs slightly moistened with the dry white wine. Rub the birds outside, thoroughly, with the oil from the artichoke hearts supplemented by ½ cup of olive oil, place in a roasting pan, put a pinch of oregano over each breast, split a clove of garlic and put it in the bottom of the roasting pan, and put in a 450-degree oven for five minutes. Meanwhile add the remainder of the olive oil to the saucepan with the white wine. After five minutes reduce the oven to 300 degrees, and, basting *frequently* with wine-oil mixture, cook for another 15 minutes, or until quail are tender. Remove to serving platter and eat immediately, along with saffron rice, baked zuccini squash, and a tossed green salad. The rest of the bottle of dry white wine should accompany it, if the cook has not finished it off. After the breasts have been sliced, quail, like the leaves of the artichoke and the finger of asparagus, should be eaten with the fingers. The artichoke and olive does *something* — don't ask me what. But try it.

Quail Gallo

Requirements

8 quail
8 small artichoke hearts in oil
8 large pitted olives
1 cup of browned breadcrumbs
1½ cups of dry white wine (Lacrima Christi)
8 small pinches of oregano
1 clove of garlic
½ cup of olive oil
salt
pepper

Quail in Aspic

This is one of the Gourmet and Wine Club recipes that is one of the most impressive you could hope to see, and I can testify that it took some time to scale it down to family size. Not only is it delicious, it is imposing to view. It can be turned out, however, by anyone with rudimentary knowledge of cooking and the ability to follow simple directions.

Requirements

6 quail
6 artichoke hearts (canned)
6 celery hearts (canned)
6 mushroom caps
6 giant olives
3 hard-boiled eggs
8 sprigs of parsley
1 egg
1 quart of chicken stock
4 stalks of celery
2 carrots
½ pound of butter
1 clove of garlic
1 lemon
½ teaspoon of rosemary
¼ teaspoon of chervil
2½ tablespoons of gelatin
salt
pepper
1 cup of white wine

HOW TO COOK

In a large kettle place 1 quart of chicken stock, 1 cup of dry white wine, 4 sprigs of parsley, 4 stalks of celery, 2 diced carrots, 1 cup of water, ½ teaspoon of rosemary, ¼ teaspoon of chervil, salt and pepper to taste (1 teaspoon of salt, ¼ teaspoon of pepper), and bring to a boil, then reduce heat to a simmer and place lid on kettle. In a skillet melt ¼ pound of butter. Rub six quail inside and out with salt and pepper and lightly brown in the butter. Remove quail and place to one side. Brown six fresh mushroom caps in the butter, remove and place to one side. When the stock has simmered for one hour, remove, strain through a sieve, and return to kettle, add browned quail and cook for 30 minutes. Add the six mushroom caps and cook for 5 minutes. Remove the quail and mushroom caps from the stock and put to one side. Allow the stock to cool slightly, skim off *all* the fat, and add the white of one egg and the shells of the egg. Boil for two minutes, remove from the fire, strain through cheesecloth and add the juice of one lemon and 2½ table-spoons of gelatin. In a large flat mold arrange the following in a pleasant pattern: 6 quail, 6 artichoke hearts, 6 celery hearts, 6 mushroom caps, 6 giant olives, 3 hard-boiled eggs cut in half, leaves of four sprigs of parsley. Slowly and carefully pour the clarified stock over these arranged items in the mold, then place in the refrigerator. When the aspic has "set" and you are ready to serve, place the mold on a large platter (platter on top), quickly turn, then cover mold for a few seconds with a dishtowel wrung out in hot water. This will release the aspic. If your arrangement is good, it will be a work of art, and even better to eat. Of course it's a lot of work! An excellent sauce can be prepared with much less effort. In a mixing bowl place one cup of mayonaise, 2 pinches of powdered dill, 1 pinch of thyme, 2 tablespoons of lemon juice, 2 teaspoons of paprika, ¼ teaspoon of onion juice, ¼ teaspoon of basil, salt and pepper. Beat with a whisk until blended. Surround the aspic with lettuce, radishes and hearts of celery. The preparation of this aspic is arduous but *not* difficult.

Dave Roberts of Cincinnati, who writes about travel, shooting, fishing and food, enjoys all four, is a fair fisherman, an excellent shot and enjoys a reputation as a chef, insists that this is as fine a method of preparing bobwhite as you can find from Ohio to the mouth of the Mississippi. This, he implies, means there is no finer method. As he is willing to admit that Smitty's method of preparing teal is "right up at the top," I feel some space should be devoted to Broiled Quail Roberts.

HOW TO COOK

Split six quail down the spine and flatten. In a saucepan melt ¼ pound of butter and pour half of it off into a cup. To the butter in the saucepan add 1 split shallot, sauté until brown then remove and throw away. Sauté six mushroom caps in the butter until lightly browned, remove and put to one side. Chop 3 chicken livers and sauté in the remaining butter in the saucepan until browned (about 5 minutes over a low flame), add ½ cup of dry red wine, ¼ teaspoon of chervil, salt and pepper, and simmer until wine is almost absorbed, then mash livers to a paste. Rub the split quail inside and outside with salt and pepper and place breast-up in a shallow roasting pan, first rubbing them thoroughly with melted butter. Place under a preheated broiler, withdrawing frequently to baste with butter. After ten to twelve minutes check for tenderness, and if tender place a mushroom cap over the breast of each quail and return to the broiler for 2 minutes. Meanwhile, spread six squares of toast with the chicken liver paste, sprinkling a few drops of lemon juice over each. Remove the quail from the broiler, place on square of liver-toast, and serve. Simple, quick, but delicious.

Broiled Quail Roberts

Requirements
6 quail
¼ pound of butter
½ cup of dry red wine
1 shallot
¼ teaspoon of chervil
6 mushroom caps
6 squares of toast
3 chicken livers
salt
pepper
1 lemon

Sautéed Quail Soskice

Requirements

6 quail
⅙ pound of butter
1 sprig of dill (¼ teaspoon
    of powdered dill)
2 sprigs of rosemary
    (¼ teaspoon of
    dry rosemary)
1 cup of dry white wine
¼ cup of port
1 tablespoon of olive oil
1 shallot
3 tablespoons of Espagnol
    sauce (or same amount
    Velouté sauce)
salt
pepper

Victor Soskice, who can prepare game with a Russian, French, Hungarian or American accent, has a simple but diverting recipe for these small birds that would charm any palate. His small dinners are always fully attended, for in addition to his personal charm he has a touch with the skillet that is unusual. Being a New Yorker he has a source of fresh herbs, and you can find his tall, spare form wandering through the foreign markets almost any day.

HOW TO COOK

In a large skillet melt ⅙ pound of butter and add 1 tablespoon of olive oil. Split a shallot into three or four slices and brown in skillet, then remove and throw away. Rub six quail with salt and pepper, then brown well in the skillet, moving the birds in the hot butter-oil frequently to insure even browning. Add one cup of dry white wine, 1 sprig of dill, 2 sprigs of rosemary, place cover on skillet and reduce flame to medium. Cook until tender, then remove to a warming oven. Add 3 tablespoons of Espagnol sauce, stir thoroughly, add ¼ cup of port, stir until gravy thickens, then pour over the quail. Magnificent!

This is a rather exotic method of preparing quail, but it was praised highly at an anniversary dinner of the Gourmet and Wine Club. It is an impressive as well as delicious dish, and not difficult to prepare.

Quail Madeira

HOW TO COOK

In a saucepan place 1½ cups of Madeira, add ½ cup of small raisins and 3 cloves, bring to a boil, then barely simmer for five minutes. In a small mixing bowl place 1 cup of cooked white rice, sprinkle with two pinches of powdered ginger, 1 teaspoon of orange peel grated fine, 1 tablespoon of melted butter. Strain the raisins from the Madeira, remove the cloves, put the Madeira to one side, then add the raisins to the mixing bowl with the rice, nuts and herbs. Blend this thoroughly and with it stuff each quail. Melt ¼ pound of butter in a saucepan and roll each stuffed quail in the butter until coated, then place the birds in a shallow roasting pan and put in a 450-degree oven for five minutes. Pour the Madeira into the saucepan with the remaining butter, add the juice of one orange and stir. After the quail have roasted for 5 minutes at 450 degrees, reduce the oven to 300 degrees and cook for 25 minutes, basting frequently with the Madeira-butter-orange basting, saving about a quarter-cup of this fluid. Remove the quail to a warming oven, place the roasting pan on the stove over a medium flame, add the saved basting, salt and pepper to taste, and stir until a gravy forms. Place the quail in a chafing dish, pour the gravy over them, and wait until steam rises from the chafing dish over the alcohol flame. Pour ½ cup of cognac over the quail, bring the rim of the chafing dish near the alcohol burner, and serve the birds blazing. If you think crêpes Suzette are impressive, try this one.

Requirements

8 quail
1 cup of cooked white rice
⅔ cup of chopped pecans
½ cup of dried raisins
2 pinches of powdered
    ginger
1½ cups of Madeira
1 orange
3 cloves
¼ pound of butter
½ cup of cognac
salt
pepper

Quail Casserole Georgia

Requirements
6 quail
1½ cups of chicken stock
12 very small white onions
12 potato balls
¼ teaspoon of rosemary
2 pinches of thyme
1 pinch of tarragon
1 carrot
1 cup of heavy cream
¼ pound of butter
1 cup of button
    mushrooms
salt
pepper

This came from the outskirts of Macon, where these small birds are guarded, appreciated, and carefully prepared. I am more than ashamed that I can't give credit to the host on this particular occasion, but everything was confused except the dinner. I copied the recipe from a dog-eared copybook in the big farm kitchen, where it was written down in what is described as "copperplate" script. I was stationed at Camp Wheeler, a few miles from Macon, at the time, and the host happened to be an acquaintance of a brother officer who was a "Georgia boy." In my own defense, I have written several letters in an attempt to learn the name of my host, but to date have had no success. The confusion mentioned was the result of a general's lady breaking her toe on the veranda shortly before dinner. There was no doctor in the house.

HOW TO COOK

In a saucepan place 3 cups of salted water and 12 tiny white onions, bring to a boil, put a lid on the pan, and simmer for 15 minutes. Drain off the water and add to the onions in the saucepan 1 grated carrot, 12 potato balls (shaped from a large potato with a curved cutter), and 1½ cups of chicken stock. Bring to a boil and simmer for 10 minutes. Melt ¼ pound of butter in a skillet. Split six quail lengthwise, rub with salt and pepper and dust lightly with flour. Sauté the quail until lightly browned in the butter, remove and arrange in the bottom of an earthenware casserole. Sprinkle the quail with ¼ teaspoon of rosemary, 2 pinches of thyme and 1 pinch of tarragon, and over them pour the onions, potatoes and stock from the saucepan. Place the cover on the casserole and put in a 350-degree oven for 15 mintues. Remove the cover, add 1 cup of button mushrooms and 1 cup of heavy cream. Replace the cover and cook for another 15 minutes in 350-degree oven. Remove and serve. A friend tried this recipe but failed to simmer the onions in salt water before simmering them in the chicken stock. This seemed, he explained, an unnecessary step. It wasn't. The flavor of onions predominated. Prepared according to directions, they do not. The casserole can be prepared (without mushrooms and cream) several hours in advance. A half-hour before dinner pop it in the oven, add the mushrooms and cream when directed, and you can spend more time having cocktails with your guests. This serves four persons nicely.

This dish was the result, admittedly, of several experiments by Benson Dalbert of New York, who was an exponent of the "pinch-of-this and pinch-of-that" school, but who kept a careful record of the pinches. He claims that he has, personally, prepared quail in more than forty ways, eventually settling upon this one. Its excellence cannot be denied, and it is *almost* as good when dried herbs are substituted for the fresh.

HOW TO COOK

In a saucepan place 1 cup of chicken stock and ½ cup of water, 1 sprig of dill, 2 sprigs of rosemary, ½ cup of chopped celery, ¼ teaspoon of salt, bring to a boil, reduce heat to a simmer and put lid on pan. Simmer for 15 minutes, strain, and put stock to one side. Split six quail lengthwise, rub with salt and pepper, dust with flour. In a large skillet melt ¼ pound of butter and add two chopped shallots. When shallots are lightly browned (2 minutes), add the quail and brown them well. Pour in the stock, add 1 tablespoon of chopped parsley, place a lid on the skillet, and simmer for 15 minutes over a low flame. Add 1 wineglass of sherry and simmer for additional 5 minutes. Add 1 cup of sour cream, freshly ground black pepper and stir contents for two minutes over a low flame, gradually adding 1½ teaspoons of paprika. Remove to serving platter.

Quail Paprika

Requirements
6 quail
¼ pound of butter
2 shallots
1 cup of chicken stock
1 wineglass of dry sherry
1 sprig of dill (2 pinches of powdered dill)
2 sprigs of rosemary (¼ teaspoon dried rosemary)
½ cup of chopped celery with leaves
1 tablespoon of chopped parsley
1 cup of sour cream
salt
freshly ground black pepper
1½ teaspoons of paprika

4

Woodcock

FOR MORE THAN a thousand years the records of the hunt and the kitchen exalt one game bird above all others. That bird is the woodcock. To the average gourmet, if a gourmet is ever "average," only one other game bird even approaches the woodcock in flavor, and that bird is almost similar in appearance and feeding habits — the snipe. Both birds have a flavor that can be matched by no other fowl, wild or domestic, but of the two the woodcock is unquestionably preferred.

Both birds are migratory, both are protected by federal law, and the open-hunting season is of short duration in the states where it is opened at all. Bag limits are low and the birds are far from plentiful, so in addition to being precious, they are rare. With the exception of perhaps a dozen exceptional markets throughout the United States, where woodcock from Europe may be obtained, the only source of supply to the gourmet is through the generosity of a hunting friend. These friendships are assiduously cultivated.

Being a small bird, the preparation of the woodcock requires more attention to detail and time than the larger bird. There are certain definite rules which should be followed in this preparation, and while some of them might be termed "chores," they are important. First, there is the initial preparation. Unless the woodcock is to be eaten the day it is killed, it should be hung in a cooling room where the temperature ranges between 40 and 45 degrees. If placed in a refrigerator, the birds should *not* be confined in a bag or container. Secondly, although many consider that the small game bird can be prepared with less effort by skinning, rather than plucking, this practice should *not* be followed with woodcock. The bird should be *dry plucked*. Thirdly, another bad practice is that of drawing small game birds by slitting them up the spine. The woodcock should be drawn in a manner similar to that of larger fowl, namely by making a small cut above the vent and removing the viscera through this opening. It is more difficult, quite true, but rewarding when the time comes to eat the bird. The smaller the orifice for drawing, the less chance there is that the bird will dry in cooking.

You can save approximately fifteen minutes per bird by doing things the easy way, but the price you pay for this speed is all out of proportion to the value of the time involved. You are *never* going to have enough woodcock, so make certain you get the full enjoyment from the few you have.

When the bird has been plucked and drawn, and the tiny heart, liver and gizzard put to one side, wipe the stomach cavity out with a dry cloth. Do *not* slosh it around in a pan of salt water. Keep it *dry*. No item of game has ever been improved by soaking in water, the woodcock least of all.

If you decide to prepare birds for the deep-freeze, place no more than two in one of the plastic envelopes, and be certain that *all* of the air has been withdrawn from the plastic envelope before the end is sealed. The woodcock can safely be held in the deep-freeze for a period of three or four months, if properly stored. And when the time arrives to withdraw the birds for cooking, leave them in the plastic containers until they have thawed. I prefer to transfer them to the refrigerator and give them 24 hours to thaw.

The average person will find no trouble in disposing of two woodcock, but my personal practice where this bird is concerned is to give them one, building up the arrival with a soup, and providing even a somewhat heavier assortment of hors d'oeuvres than normal, to insure that no one leaves the table hungry. For this reason the recipes given will be for four birds. If only two will be at the table, perhaps generosity will sway you to provide two woodcock each.

It is a practical impossibility to prepare any game bird with more ease than the method now to be given. Unfortunately, it is not always possible to be in a position to carry out this method of preparation. During the aftermath of World War II, I was among a number of other impatient officers who were held over for many months at Allied Force Headquarters. Among the group was one General D.E.P. Hodgson of the Welsh Guards, who was and is one of the most persistent sportsmen I have ever encountered. During the course of the war, when time came for a brief period of "Rest and Recuperation," the two of us rested by hunting the Italian quail, waterfowl, snipe and woodcock. During the holdover period, while stationed at Caserta, we had more time to indulge in this healthy activity, and we did not waste it.

The method followed by General Hodgson in preparing woodcock for the table was, as I stated, extremely simple. The method of eating was even simpler, as it involved only the use of the fingers. It is a method of preparation I would follow only on the same day the birds were killed. The General, however, insisted they were much better after having been "hung" for a few days. Not for me!!!

On the return trip from the shooting ground the General and I sat on the tailgate of his Army "P.U.," each of us selected two woodcock, and began scattering feathers along the route. If it had been an especially strenuous day we even picked three apiece. By the time we returned to his quarters all the birds were carefully dry-plucked, even the pin feathers had been removed. When the car drew up in front of his place, his batman turned up the fire and placed on it an oversize iron kettle half-filled with olive oil. The four (or six) woodcock were rubbed with salt and pepper, and when the blue smoke began to rise from the olive oil, they were dropped in the kettle, where they bobbed and ducked around like doughnuts. In about five or six minutes they were ready, and Lucullus never enjoyed a finer repast. The birds were eaten like an ear of corn, with the fingers, and with fresh Italian bread and a tossed green salad, no one could have asked for more. Prepared in this manner, the heat seems to form the viscera into a tiny hard ball, and the hearts and livers are cooked to a turn. The interior of the stomach cavity is as clean as the proverbial whistle. We left nothing but the small ball of viscera and an assortment of clean-picked tiny bones. We prepared snipe and quail in the same manner, and once even tried teal and found them excellent. However, as I pointed out, this method is acceptable, at least so far as I am concerned, only when the birds are *fresh*.

Woodcock Hodgson

Woodcock Augusta

Requirements
4 woodcock
¾ cup of browned
    breadcrumbs
½ cup of preserved
    blueberries
1 ounce of cognac
1 cup of dry white wine
⅙ pound of sweet butter
2 pinches of chervil
1 pinch of tarragon
1 cup of heavy cream
1 shallot
1 stalk of celery
salt
freshly ground
    black pepper

At least twenty years ago I was woodcock hunting in Maine, where you find some of the finest covers ever roamed by a man with a dog. I was visiting, and hunting with, the late John Burns, only a stone's throw from Merrymeeting Bay. John had, at that time, been retired for several years, and he spent his time hunting waterfowl and woodcock and fishing for trout and salmon, and when there was no activity in these sports, he concentrated on culinary experimentation, at which he was exceptionally proficient. The method of preparing Woodcock Augusta was his own, but I have found no other method that was finer.

HOW TO COOK

Rub four woodcock inside and out with salt and pepper. In a mixing bowl place ¾ cup of browned breadcrumbs, ½ cup of drained preserved blueberries, and one ounce of cognac. Stir gently until berries and breadcrumbs are mingled, then stir in two tablespoons of heavy cream and two tablespoons of dry white wine, which should give the dressing the proper consistency for stuffing. Stuff the four woodcock with this and sew the openings carefully. Put to one side. In a small saucepan melt ⅙ pound of butter. In another saucepan place 1 cup of dry white wine (less two tablespoons), 1 minced shallot, one minced stalk of celery, 1 pinch of tarragon and 2 pinches of chervil. Steep for ten minutes over low flame, strain, and put liquor to one side. Roll the four woodcock in the melted butter until thoroughly coated, then place them in a shallow roasting pan (small one) and put in an oven preheated to 400 degrees for 5 minutes. After five minutes reduce the heat to 300 degrees and baste alternately with herb-wine and melted butter, and when this is used up, with drippings. After 25 minutes in the 300-degree oven the birds should be tender. Test, and if necessary give them another 5 minutes. Remove the birds to a platter and a warming oven. Place the pan over a low flame, add 1 cup of heavy cream (less two tablespoons), stir and scrape until thick gravy is formed. Pour this gravy over the birds and serve. The stuffing seems to keep the birds properly moist, and the combined blueberries and cognac enhances the natural flavor of the woodcock. This is truly a dish for the most exacting gourmet, let alone a mere king.

On the St. John River in New Brunswick, a province noted for its fine hunting and fishing but not, alas, for its cuisine, there is a small hunting lodge not far from Gagetown. At the time I hunted there it was operated by Thomas Scovil, who has since moved to the States. Tom, unhappily familiar with the culinary reputation of his province, had done considerable scouring to find a cook who would prevent him from being tarred with the common brush. He was successful. Products of the Scovil kitchen were far more efficacious than a better mousetrap, so far as luring guests to the door of the manor. Their preparation of woodcock, of which the surrounding covers provided a substantial number, was well worth a long trip.

HOW TO COOK

Rub four woodcock inside and out with salt and pepper and dust with flour. In large saucepan melt ¼ pound of butter, then add two green onions chopped very fine, 1 carrot chopped fine, ¼ teaspoon of basil, 2 pinches of tarragon. Stir constantly in the butter over a low flame for five minutes, add the woodcock, and sauté until lightly browned. Remove woodcock to an earthenware casserole. To the contents of the saucepan add one medium-sized apple, peeled, cored and diced fine, ½ cup of chicken stock, 1 cup of dry white wine and ½ bay leaf. Simmer for 30 minutes, then strain and pour over woodcock in casserole. Add one cup of sour cream, place cover on casserole, and put in oven preheated to 350 degrees. Cook for 45 minutes, remove cover from casserole and cook for an additional ten minutes. Remove to chafing dish and serve. The gravy will be thick, rich and aromatic, and the woodcock will have lost none of their distinctive flavor. For a larger group, even for a buffet, it is merely necessary to double the recipe. With wild rice, a green vegetable, a tossed green salad, and herb rolls, it will insure you an enviable reputation as a host. *Or hostess.* (Tom's cook was a woman!)

Woodcock St. John

Requirements

4 woodcock
4 tablespoons of flour
¼ pound of butter
¼ teaspoon of basil
2 pinches of tarragon
2 green onions (scallions)
1 cup of dry white wine
1 carrot
½ cup of chicken stock
½ bay leaf
1 medium-sized apple
salt
freshly ground
    black pepper
1 cup of sour cream

Woodcock Dominick & Louis

Requirements
4 woodcock
4 fresh mushrooms
1 cup of dry white wine
½ cup of toasted
    breadcrumbs
1 2-ounce can paté
    de foie gras
1 ounce of dry vermouth
1 pinch of marjoram
1 pinch of chervil
1 pinch of tarragon
1 lemon
½ cup of sour cream
½ cup of olive oil
2 tablespoons of butter
salt
freshly ground
    black pepper
2 shallots

The small French restaurant once known to a knowing group as "Dominick and Louis" is no longer in existence. It did not die out for lack of clientele, but because of a matter of climate. "The sinuses of Louis," Dominick explained, "cannot combat this climate." On one occasion I happened to be in possession of four plump woodcock but not in possession of a kitchen. To be in New York City with one and without the other is an unfortunate situation, but one which Louis relieved. I was an "old customer," and since he could not prepare game for sale, he would do it for friendship. I rounded up one kindred spirit and we settled down in a corner table. This was the result.

HOW TO COOK

Rub four woodcock inside and out with salt and pepper and put to one side. In a saucepan melt two tablespoons of butter and add 2 shallots minced fine, one pinch of tarragon and four fresh mushrooms diced in ¼-inch cubes. Sauté until lightly browned, about five minutes over a low flame. Stir in ½ cup of toasted breadcrumbs, 1 ounce of dry vermouth, salt and pepper, and enough white wine to give proper consistency. Stuff the four woodcock with this dressing, sew openings carefully and put to one side. In a saucepan place remainder of the cup of wine, one pinch of marjoram, one pinch of chervil, the juice of one lemon, and ½ cup of olive oil. Bring to a boil, then reduce flame and simmer for ten minutes. Dip the woodcock in this basting, place in a shallow roasting pan, and put in an oven preheated to 450 degrees. After ten minutes reduce oven heat to 350 degrees, baste with wine-herb-oil-lemon stock and cook for another 30 minutes, basting *frequently* with stock, and, when stock is gone, with drippings. After 30 minutes remove woodcock to a platter and warming oven, place roasting pan on top of stove over low flame and stir ½ cup of sour cream into drippings, scraping pan. When gravy has thickened pour over woodcock and serve, first having placed each woodcock on a square of toast spread with *pâté de foie gras*. Louis pointed out that he had served woodcock prepared *comme ça* to ROYALTY, for which he was complimented. We also complimented.

This one was practically "sneaked" from the kitchen of Bob Russell, who, some may insist, contributed largely to this volume. I would be much more grateful had it not been necessary to do so much prying and bribing in order to get some of his so-called "secrets." It was rather surprising, knowing Russell, to eat woodcock prepared in this manner, but it apppears that this is one of the few birds that he does not consider suited for cooking over charcoal. "No matter how lightly you handle them," he admits, "they tend to lose some juice and flavor over hot coals."

Woodcock Pilau

HOW TO COOK

Rub four woodcock inside and out with salt and pepper and put to one side. In a large saucepan melt ⅙ pound of butter, add one clove of garlic split in half. Sauté until garlic is brown, then remove and throw away. Add one minced shallot, sauté lightly for two minutes, then brown the four woodcock in the butter. Remove the woodcock when lightly browned and place in earthenware casserole. To the butter and shallot in the saucepan add one cup of white wine and two cups of chicken stock, 1 diced shallot, 3 stalks of celery minced fine, 2 carrots minced, 1 pinch of basil, ¼ teaspoon of powdered dill, 2 pinches of chervil, 2 dashes of Tabasco sauce, salt and pepper. Bring to a boil, then reduce flame and simmer for 30 minutes. Strain, pushing vegeables through a course sieve, and put to one side. Wash thoroughly one cup of wild rice, then put in a pot of boiling salt water for five minutes. Drain off rice, wash thoroughly in cold water, drain and arrange around woodcock in casserole. Pour the strained stock over the woodcock and rice, place cover on casserole, and put in 350-degree oven for 40 minutes. Remove the cover from the casserole and return to the 350-degree oven for another 10 minutes. Serve in casserole. If prepared according to directions the grains of wild rice will be separate, and will have absorbed most of the stock. All of the natural flavor of the woodcock seems to be retained. Care should be taken to use a casserole small enough to permit the rice to *cover* the woodcock at least ½ inch. Bob served this with tomatoes stewed with one clove of garlic, zuccini squash and hearts of lettuce with Roquefort cheese dressing.

Requirements
4 woodcock
1 cup of wild rice
2 shallots
3 stalks of celery
2 carrots
1 cup of dry white wine
2 cups of chicken stock
    (or chicken consommé)
1 pinch of basil
¼ teaspoon powdered dill
2 pinches of chervil
⅙ pound of butter
2 dashes of Tabasco sauce
salt and pepper
1 clove of garlic

Woodcock Guido

Requirements

4 woodcock
3 small onions
⅛ pound of butter
1 cup of dry vermouth
2 tablespoons of Marsala
½ cup of mushrooms
½ cup of pitted green
    olives
¾ cup of browned
    breadcrumbs
1 pinch of savory
1 lemon
salt
freshly ground
    black pepper
4 slices of toast

Just off the Via Appia near Garigliano there was a small restaurant operated by one Guido Ferrara who, before the war and his firm convictions drove him from Rome, was a chef at one of the finest Roman restaurants. The small restaurant he operated at the end of the war provided him with a meager living, but a happy one. As the marshes where I hunted were near, I often brought him ducks, snipe or woodcock to prepare, and when I came to know him I tried to gather in a half-dozen of the local "coots" or mud hens that he seemed to enjoy. I was firm in my refusal to try one of these birds, although he urged me many times. I had eaten coot at home, and was not interested in trying it again, especially with better wildfowl available. His method of preparing woodcock was not Italian in character, although some of the ingredients were popular in their cookery. The recipe, he insisted, had been evolved by him during his Roman period.

HOW TO COOK

In a saucepan melt half of the ⅛ pound of butter, add three small onions chopped fine, ½ cup of diced mushrooms, and sauté for five minutes over a medium flame; then add 2 tablespoons of Marsala, 1 pinch of savory, salt and pepper, and stir well. Stir in ¾ cup of browned breadcrumbs and ½ cup of chopped and pitted green olives. Rub the woodcock inside and out with salt and pepper, then stuff with the dressing, sewing the opening carefully. Rub the birds thoroughly with the remainder of the ⅛ pound of butter and place in a shallow roasting pan, then in an oven preheated to 400 degrees, for 10 minutes. Meanwhile put one cup of dry vermouth and the juice of one lemon in a saucepan and bring to a boil. Remove the saucepan from the fire and baste the woodcock with the hot vermouth-lemon mixture. After ten minutes reduce the oven to 350 degrees. Basting frequently, cook the woodcock for twenty minutes in the 350-degree oven. Remove the woodcock to a warming oven and place the roasting pan over a low flame, add ½ cup of water and stir and scrape the pan until a thick gravy results. Place the four slices of toast in this gravy until it is absorbed. Place the toast, gravy side up, on a platter and place a woodcock on each slice.

This recipe came from the Gourmet and Wine Club and would have been a prime favorite had there been an adequate supply of woodcock, but unfortunately birds were available not more than twice a year. It is not difficult to prepare, and is rewarding.

Breast of Woodcock

HOW TO COOK

Carefully (preferably with poultry shears) cut the breasts (leaving breastbone) from four woodcock and put to one side. Chop the remainder of the woodcock and the livers, hearts and gizzards, and place in a saucepan with the following: 2 tablespoons of butter, 2 diced carrots, 2 stalks of celery diced fine, 3 diced shallots, 1 minced clove of garlic, ¼ teaspoon of tarragon, 4 sprigs of parsley, 1½ cups of chicken stock and ½ cup of dry sherry. Simmer over a low flame for one hour, or until stock is reduced to about one cup. Remove woodcock bones and force stock and vegetables through a sieve. If more than one cup results, continue to simmer until stock is reduced to this quantity. Rub remainder of the butter on the woodcock breasts, first rubbing them lightly with salt and pepper, place them in a shallow pan and put under the broiler (2 inches from flame) until lightly browned. Place breasts in a small, shallow earthenware casserole, pour the stock over them and place the lid on the casserole. Cook in a 350-degree oven for 30 minutes, then remove woodcock breasts to a platter in warming oven. Blend ½ cup of heavy cream with the drippings remaining in the casserole, pour over the breasts and serve.

Requirements
4 woodcock
⅙ pound of butter
2 carrots
2 stalks of celery
1½ cups of chicken stock
½ cup of dry sherry
1 clove of garlic
¼ teaspoon of tarragon
4 sprigs of parsley
½ cup of heavy cream
salt
freshly ground
    black pepper
3 shallots

5
Pigeons and Doves

IN THE MATTER of size, flavor and texture there is little difference between the pigeon and the dove. Both have a tendency to greater flavor and succulence in some areas, and a marked lack of both in others. This is a matter of the quantity and quality of the natural food, rather than a natural characteristic.

Neither of these game birds is "fat," so both are inclined to be dry, stringy, and poorly flavored if improperly prepared. I have encountered a number of these birds that had been prepared by cooks who handled them as they would the fat squabs purchased from their butcher. This, of course, is a serious mistake, for the wild bird is not only less tender but has only a small percentage of the fat possessed by the squab.

Because of their serious decrease in numbers, both birds are on the protected list, and open seasons as well as the bag limits are much lower than they were in the proverbial "good old days." As the use of these birds decreased, so did the knowledge of their preparation. Both birds have a firm place on the gourmet's list, however, although they are available only to the hunter or to the man who happens to have a good friend who is a capable shot and possessed of a certain amount of generosity when it comes to the bag.

The passenger pigeon, now extinct, once provided a source of winter meat for thousands of rural householders, for the birds moved down the Atlantic and East-Central states in flights of millions. Many farmers salted down hundreds of these birds after the migration passed, and pigeons were shipped to public markets by the barrel.

I have heard many express their dissatisfaction with both pigeons and doves as a table delicacy, but in every instance this was the result of improper preparation. Both birds should be hung in a cool place, preferably a cooling or curing room, for at least three days, and there is a difference of opinion as to whether they should be drawn prior to this hanging. Unless the stomach cavity is to be filled, my own opinion is that the drawing should be postponed until they are prepared for the table. One man I know insists upon drawing them first, but he inserts half a peeled apple in the stomach cavity during the curing period. Unles you like "high" game, which most Americans do not, I suggest making three days the maximum period for curing. This applies not only to the pigeon and dove, but to other game birds.

This recipe caused me a lot of trouble. Many years ago I was quail shooting with one George Kearse in Bamberg County, South Carolina. The weather was dry, windy and unusually cold, and the quail joined the dogs in failing to cooperate. Then came an invitation from a nearby plantation owner to a dove shoot, which we would have accepted even had the quail shooting been twice as productive. "Bring me back a good bait of doves and I'll have the girl make you a purleau you'll remember," George suggested. George Kearse was an untiring speller. When he introduced me to a local neighbor he would proclaim: "Mr. C-a-m-p meet Mr. E-m-e-r-s-o-n." He spelled out every name. He could not, unfortunately, spell purleau. A family conference on the subject brought out suggestions such as p-e-r-l-e-w, p-u-r-l-u, p-u-r-l-o-w, p-u-r-l-e-a-u, etc., etc. I settled on the last as being the most probable. After having eaten the purleau and found it good, I ran the recipe in my column. During the next six weeks I received letters from a dozen states, adding to the list of suggested spelling and pronunciation. No one, however, complained as to the quality of the recipe.

Dove Purleau

Requirements
8 doves or pigeons
½ pound of butter
1 cup of canned tomatoes
2 small onions
1 teaspoon of powdered marjoram
1 cup of flour
½ teaspoon of basil
1 clove of garlic
4 cups of chicken stock
salt
pepper
2 cups of white rice

HOW TO COOK

Place one cup of flour and 1 teaspoon of powdered marjoram, salt and pepper in a large brown-paper bag. Split 8 doves or pigeons down the spine and breast. Shake the half-birds in the paper bag with the flour and marjoram until well dusted, then put to one side. Melt ½ pound of butter in a large kettle over a medium flame, add one split clove of garlic and brown it well, then remove garlic and throw away. Brown the birds *well* but quickly in the butter, then remove them to a warming oven. Wash and scrub two cups of rice, then dry it as thoroughly as possible. Prepare 1 cup of chopped, canned tomatoes, without the juice, and dice 2 small onions. Brown the onions in the butter, add the cup of tomatoes and stir for two minutes. Add the two cups of rice and continue stirring in the butter until the rice is slightly browned. Prepare in advance 4 cups of chicken stock to which has been added ½ teaspoon of basil. Place the halved doves or pigeons in the kettle, stir them with the rice, then add the four cups of chicken stock. Bring to a boil, stirring constantly, then reduce the heat to a minimum simmer, place a lid on the kettle, and *do not disturb for 25 minutes.* Remove from the stove, stir the contents carefully, place in a large, deep platter, and serve. The rice will be just right and the birds tender and juicy. Do not fret if a thin layer of rice has adhered to the bottom of the pan. With this George's cook served creamed cabbage, beet greens, hot biscuits, and a lettuce salad with sugar and vinegar dressing. We drank a few gallons of medium-hard cider with it.

Dove Casserole Jennings

Requirements

6 doves (or pigeons)
2 cups of sliced fresh
    mushrooms
2 cups of sliced raw potato
1 cup of thinly sliced carrot
1 cup of thinly sliced onion
1 cup of strong chicken
    broth
1 cup of white wine
¼ pound of butter
1 teaspoon of powdered
    marjoram
1½ cups of heavy cream
salt
freshly ground
    black pepper
1 clove of garlic

One of the orginal members of the Gourmet and Wine Club, C.E.M. Jennings, was a specialist in game cookery. On no occasion, so far as I can remember, would he accept a dinner assignment unless the dish for which he was responsible involved some form of game. He kept this particular recipe a well-guarded secret for several years, but finally succumbed to a trade which involved a twenty-pound "chunk" of moose meat. It was worth it, especially as I had one entire moose (minus head, tail, hide and feet) in a freeze locker. When writing my column on the moose safari I had very foolishly mentioned that the animal had reached extremely advanced age. When the meat had been properly cured, packaged and frozen, I offered bits and pieces to friends, who greeted these offers with knowing smiles and firm refusals. Jennings, fortunately, did not take the newspaper for which I slaved, so he was willing to trade for the large section of hind-quarter.

HOW TO COOK

Melt ¼ pound of butter in a large skillet. Add one split clove of garlic, brown well, then remove and throw away. Rub six doves, split lengthwise, with salt and freshly ground black pepper, dust lightly with flour, and sauté in butter until well browned, using a fire as hot as possible without burning. Remove doves and place in a warming oven. In an earthenware casserole brushed with some of the butter from the skillet, place a layer of thinly sliced onion, a layer of carrot, a layer of potato and a layer of mushrooms, then arrange the doves on top. Sprinkle a pinch of powdered marjoram on each layer. Over the doves pour half of the remaining butter in the skillet, then cover with layers of onion, carrot, potato and mushroom. Add salt and pepper to taste, then pour 1 cup of strong chicken broth and one cup of white wine over the contents of the casserole, add remainder of butter, put on the cover, and cook in a 350-degree oven for 20 minutes. Remove cover, add 1½ cups of heavy cream, replace cover and cook for another 30 minutes in 300-degree oven. This is a magnificent buffet supper dish, for all you need in addition to the main dish is hot herb rolls and a tossed salad. It is *not* a dish for those concerned with any type of reducing diet.

Lucille Purser, who operates the Carolinian at Nag's Head, on the Outer Banks, sets one of the finest tables in North Carolina, which, among other things, undoubtedly accounts for the tremendous success of that hostelry. A number of wildfowlers who visit that area may be hunting at Currituck Sound, Kitty Hawk Bay, Roanoke Sound or Wanchese, but those "in the know" make their headquarters at the Carolinian, where they know the accommodations are fine and the food superb. You always get an assortment of hot breads, homemade jams and jellies, fine sweet-'tater pie, and even Yaupon Tea if you prefer it.

HOW TO COOK

In a skillet melt 1 tablespoon of butter and sauté 1 cup of good Virginia (or North Carolina) country ham chopped into ¼-inch bits. When lightly browned add one minced onion, sauté for about 1 minute, then stir in 1 cup of cooked rice and sprinkle with 2 pinches of thyme. Stuff the doves with this dressing and pin two half-slices of bacon across the breast of each dove. Place in a shallow roasting pan and put into an oven preheated to 450 degrees for ten minutes. Add salt and pepper to 1 cup of chicken stock and after reducing the oven to 300 degrees, baste the pigeons *frequently* with chicken stock for another 30 minutes. Remove doves to a warming oven, and place roasting pan over light flame, stir in 1 tablespoon of flour, then add ½ cup of chicken stock, stirring and scraping until thick gravy forms. Remove browned bacon from dove breasts, pour gravy over them and serve.

Tarheel Doves

Requirements
4 doves (or pigeons)
1 cup of cooked rice
1 cup of diced *smoked* ham
4 strips of bacon
1 tablespoon of flour
2 pinches of thyme
1 ½ cups of chicken stock
1 small onion
salt
pepper
1 tablespoon of butter

Pigeon Andros

Requirements

8 pigeons (or doves)
3 cups of cooked wild rice
1 cup of chopped
    button mushrooms
½ pint of dry white wine
1 wineglass of port
    (Madeira can be
    substituted)
½ cup of fresh lime juice
⅙ pound of butter
½ teaspoon of rosemary
2 shallots
2 pinches of thyme
salt
freshly ground
    black pepper

Smitty, who presides with a firm hand and a broad smile over the Lighthouse Club kitchen at Andros Town, in the Bahamas, has joined me in many an early-morning pigeon shoot at Coakley Town and Love Hill, two nearby "settlements." Later, I joined him in a "pigeon eat," and, as they say locally, "Mon, that Smitty can fix pigeons!" I can recall one guest at the Lighthouse Club who spent almost as much time in the kitchen as he did fishing, who ate six of these pigeons, one after the other, and stopped only at the firm insistence of his wife. Smitty promised to prepare two birds for his breakfast, when the wife would be in bed.

HOW TO COOK

In a small saucepan melt 2 tablespoons of butter and in this lightly brown two minced shallots. Add 2 pinches of thyme, salt and pepper, 1 wineglass of port and stir in 1 cup of chopped button mushrooms. Bring to a boil, remove from heat and stir in three cups of cooked wild rice. Rub eight pigeons with salt and freshly ground black pepper, inside and out. Stuff birds with wild rice, then rub birds thoroughly with butter and place in a shallow roasting pan. In a saucepan place ½ pint of dry white wine, ½ teaspoon of rosemary, ½ cup of lime juice, and the remainder of the butter. Bring to a boil and remove from heat. Place the pigeons in an oven preheated to 500 degrees for five minutes, reduce the heat to 350 degrees, and cook for 25 minutes, basting *very* frequently with the wine-lime juice-butter mixture. Baste with the drippings when this is used up. Remove the pigeons to a warming oven, place the roasting pan over a low flame and add ½ cup of water, stirring and scraping the pan until the gravy thickens. Pour over the pigeons and serve. With this Smitty served broccoli hollandaise, and sliced avocado with a dressing of lime juice, olive oil and salt and pepper, then a steamed mango pudding with brandy sauce. The chilled bottle of Tavel added a real touch.

This was a California dish evolved by a man who was convinced that Americans should be forcibly educated to the *haute cuisine*. Tom Ballard had, so far as I know, never done a day's work for pay until he was thirty-five, when he came to New York to open a restaurant and put his convictions into practice. About eight months after he opened the restaurant he was driving to the Outer Banks of North Carolina for the opening of the waterfowl season when a trailer truck swung at high speed into the lane in which he was traveling. Tom did not survive the accident. He was a meticulous and imaginative amateur chef, and was a firm crusader for "better cooking." Panned Pigeon is one of the three recipes I was fortunate enough to obtain from him.

HOW TO COOK

Split four pigeons down the breast and spine. Place them in a bowl and sprinkle them with 1 wineglass of Calvados, then brush them with this spirit until it is all absorbed. Melt ⅙ pound of butter in a skillet, dust the pigeons lightly with flour, sprinkle, *do not rub,* with salt and pepper, and sauté in the butter until browned. Remove to a warming oven. Sauté 1½ cups of sliced fresh mushrooms in the butter until browned, return the split pigeons to the skillet, add 1 teaspoon of chopped parsley, 1 pinch of ginger, 2 pinches of thyme, salt, and freshly ground black pepper, 1 cup of chicken stock and one cup of rosé wine. Bring to a boil, stir, then reduce heat to a simmer and cook with a cover on the skillet for twenty minutes, or until pigeons are tender. Blend 1 tablespoon of lemon juice with ½ cup of orange juice and pour over the contents of the skillet, stirring well. Replace the lid and simmer for five minutes, then remove the lid and simmer until liquid has reduced to thick gravy.

Panned Pigeon

Requirements
4 pigeons (or doves)
1 wineglass of Calvados
   (or applejack)
1 cup of chicken stock
1 cup of rosé wine
1½ cups of sliced fresh
   mushrooms
⅙ pound of butter
1 tablespoon of chopped
   parsley
2 pinches of thyme
1 pinch of ginger
1 tablespoon of lemon juice
½ cup of orange juice
salt
freshly ground
   black pepper

Pigeons Athena

Requirements
4 pigeons
1 cup of salt ripe olives
1 cup of white cooked rice
1 small pinch of saffron
1½ cups of dry white wine
½ teaspoon of rosemary
½ cup of olive oil
1 cup of sour cream
salt and pepper

Tom brought this recipe back from Athens, where he spent almost a year at the end of World War II. It is an excellent recipe, but calls for a bit of scurrying around for those who do not happen to live in an area where salted olives can be obtained. I have tried a substitute in the form of large, ripe olives, and while it is not *quite* the same, the difference is slight. Also, the dry wine used by Tom is the Greek wine that has a faint resinous flavor.

HOW TO COOK

Chop into quarter-inch pieces 1 cup of pitted salt ripe olives. In a saucepan place 1½ cups of white wine, 1 *small* pinch of saffron, ½ teaspoon of rosemary, the chopped olives, and bring to a boil. Reduce the flame to a simmer and cook for three minutes. Strain off the olives and retain the liquor. Blend the olives with 1 cup of rice, add freshly ground black pepper to taste, and stuff the pigeons with this dressing, sewing the openings afterward. Rub the pigeons well with olive oil and place them in a shallow roasting pan. Add the remainder of the olive oil (½ cup) to the wine-herb mixture in the saucepan. Place the pigeons in an oven that has been preheated to 450 degrees for ten minutes, reduce the heat to 300 degrees, and cook for thirty minutes, basting frequently with the olive oil-wine-herb basting. When basting fluid is used up, baste with drippings. Frequent basting is *very* important. Remove pigeons to a warming oven and place roasting pan over low flame, add 1 cup of sour cream, stir and scrape until thick gravy forms, then pour gravy over pigeons. This is one of the finest pigeon dishes ever invented. You can come close to duplicating the salt olives by adding a heaping tablespoon of salt to pitted ripe olives and putting them in the refrigerator overnight, then giving them a quick washing before chopping. Remember, *watch* that saffron (5 tendrils of dry saffron or an amount of powdered saffron the size of the head of a wooden match). With this Tom served a tremendous bowl of artichokes cooked with diced celery, fresh dill, small potatoes and olive oil. And chilled white Greek wine. Incidentally, the artichoke-celery-potato dish is magnificent served chilled.

6
Wild Turkey

THE WILD TURKEY is, unquestionably, king of all the game birds. Not merely because of its size, but because of its flavor, which is impossible to describe. It is definitely a "wild" flavor, but it is not what most people describe as "gamey." There are several strains of wild turkey that are reared on game farms, under a license, and sold as "wild turkey." These birds have no more flavor than the ordinary domestic turkey, and their major difference is that they have less fat than the run-of-the-mill domestic bird. It is the food habits of the true wild bird that provide the flavor, and for this reason special care should be taken in the preparation, to insure that this flavor is enhanced rather than diminished.

With the exception of the variations in stuffing, or dressing, there is only one method of preparing turkey that insures the retention of the full flavor, although there are two variations in method, one calling for the use of a half-bird, the other a whole bird. I will list a few of the stuffings, then the general method of preparation.

Turkey Blane

Requirements

1 pound of sweet butter
3 cups of wild rice
5 cups of dry white wine
3 cups of chicken stock
1 cup of blanched almonds
½ teaspoon of rosemary
½ teaspoon of marjoram
1 pinch of thyme
1 clove of garlic
1 dash of Tabasco sauce
salt
freshly ground
    black pepper
2 tablespoons of parsley

Gerry Blane is a Texan who ranges from Dallas to San Antonio, but spends a good part of his time in a small hunting hideaway near the Nueces River. Having spent a dozen years in Paris, it was not surprising to find that his kitchen represented more of an investment than all of the rest of his hunting lodge combined. Tinned copper pots and pans and glazed earthenware casseroles were present in all sizes and shapes, and the major task of his part-time caretaker was the watering of his shaded herb garden. Although a firm disciple of the French school of cookery in most meats and fish, he insisted that the French too often tended to "dress up game too heavily." Although he occasionally employed the stronger herbs and seasonings, he used them with real moderation, pointing out that "used with restraint, they bring out the true flavor of game." Gerry killed a lot of game during the course of a year, for he hunted in a half-dozen states. But he never wasted an ounce, and enjoyed all of it to the maximum.

HOW TO COOK

Melt ⅛ pound of butter in a saucepan over a low flame, and when it is clear add one cup of blanched almonds, stirring constantly until almonds are lightly browned. Remove almonds and put them to one side. Add one split clove of garlic to butter in saucepan, brown it, then remove and throw away. Sauté in this butter the chopped liver, heart and gizzard of the turkey. Brown over a low flame for ten minutes, then add 1 cup of white wine and 3 cups of chicken stock, ½ teaspoon of marjoram, ½ teaspoon of rosemary, 1 pinch of thyme, 1 dash of Tabasco sauce, 2 table-spoons of chopped parsley. Bring to a boil, then reduce heat to a simmer, place cover on saucepan, and allow to simmer for 10 minutes. Wash three cups of wild rice in cold water, rub grains thoroughly, then cook in 3 quarts of boiling water to which 1 teaspoon of salt is added, for five minutes. Drain and wash with cold water. Place the rice in an earthenware casserole, add salt and pepper to taste to the simmering stock, and pour stock over rice. Place lid on casserole in 350-degree oven for 30 minutes. Remove and allow to cool.

Rub the inside of the turkey thoroughly with salt and pepper. Stuff with the wild rice dressing to which the cup of browned chopped almonds has been added. Sew up the opening carefully, then rub the entire bird with sweet butter from the remaining ⅝ of a pound. Layer the breast thoroughly with the butter. Place the remainder of the butter in a saucepan, add four cups of white wine and bring to a boil. Remove from the fire for use as basting. Place the turkey in a shallow roasting pan and in an oven preheated to 450 degrees. Allow to remain in the oven at this temperature for 20 minutes. Reduce the heat to 350 degrees and baste frequently with wine-butter basting. It should cook at 350 degrees for not more than 15 minutes to the pound. Remove the turkey to a warming oven, place the roasting pan over a medium flame and add one cup of Espagnol sauce to the drippings, stirring and scraping the pan. Serve the gravy separately. With the stuffing to serve as a starch, serve a green vegetable, a salad of lettuce and orange and grapefruit sections with a tart dressing.

Wild Turkey Roche

This method was evolved by Charles Roche of the Gourmet and Wine Club, who is an active sportsman as well as an excellent amateur chef. On every occasion but two, he provided the wild turkey. He was adamant on one subject, that wild turkey demanded chestnut stuffing. His basting mixture was almost similar to that of Blane, and he agreed completely as to the use of Espagnol sauce in the gravy.

Requirements

3 cups of cooked chestnuts
1 ounce of dry sherry
1 ounce of Madeira
½ cup of chopped celery
    heart
1 teaspoon of rosemary
¾ pound of sweet butter
1 clove of garlic
2 pinches of thyme
1½ cups of ½-inch cubes
    of bread
1 tablespoon of chopped
    parsley
2 shallots
3 cups of dry white wine
½ cup of chicken stock
salt
freshly ground
    black pepper
½ cup of heavy cream
1 cup of Espagnol sauce

HOW TO COOK

In a medium-size skillet melt ¼ pound of sweet butter, add one split clove of garlic. Brown garlic, remove and throw away. Sauté in the butter 1½ cups of ½-inch cubes of white bread, stirring carefully until bread has browned, then remove to brown paper. To the butter in the skillet add 2 minced shallots, brown well over medium heat, than add ½ cup of chopped celery heart, ½ teaspoon of rosemary, salt and pepper, 1 tablespoon of chopped parsley, ½ cup of chicken stock, 2 pinches of thyme, 1 ounce of dry sherry, and ½ cup of heavy cream. Simmer over low heat for two minutes stirring constantly, then add browned bread cubes, stirring them in well. Next add 3 cups of cooked chestnuts, forming all into a dressing. Rub the inside of the turkey with 1 ounce of Madeira, stuff with dressing and sew opening carefully. Rub the entire turkey thoroughly with sweet butter, then place remaining butter in saucepan with 3 cups of dry white wine and ½ teaspoon of rosemary. Bring to a quick boil and remove from heat. Place the turkey in an oven preheated to 500 degrees for 10 minutes, reduce heat to 350 degrees and roast 15 minutes to the pound, basting frequently. When turkey has approximately 30 minutes to cook, add chopped liver, heart and gizzard to pan. When turkey is tender, remove to a warming oven, and place roasting pan over low flame on the stove. Add ½ cup of boiling water and stir and scrape pan. Add one cup of Espagnol sauce, stirring constantly until gravy thickens.

Wild Turkey Carolina

Thomas Grafton, who lives in the "mountings" of North Carolina in a patch of woods so close to the Tennessee line that he has to watch where he walks, is forced to spend "too much" of his time in Chicago earning a living. His real "living" and his real "home," he insists, are in the Tarheel State. His recipe for wild turkey stuffing is almost exactly the same as that of Charles Roche with the substitution of 3 cups of apples, in half-inch cubes, for the 3 cups of chestnuts. As a matter of fact, it is so close that I have long suspected collusion. Also, instead of using dry white wine for basting, Grafton uses 3 cups of hard cider to which has been added one wineglass of applejack. Needless to say, he is an apple man from 'way back. The result, I must admit, is not only different, but wonderful. Grafton also has a method of stuffings quail with pecans that is equally fine (see Quail).

Wild Turkey Dyer

Requirements

½ pound of butter
2 shallots
1 cup of chopped celery
2 tablespoons of chopped
    parsley
½ teaspoon of marjoram
1 teaspoon of paprika
¼ teaspoon of rosemary
2 pinches of ground cloves
1 cup of crushed pineapple
2 cups of browned
    breadcrumbs
½ cup of heavy cream
2 cups of chicken stock
salt
pepper

Judge Harry Dyer of Stuart, who is one of the most enterprising, hard-working, enthusiastic and hospitable quail enthusiasts I have ever encountered, is one of the few cooks who can turn out a fine meal under far from auspicious circumstances. He does not attempt to prepare wild turkey on his Everglades safaris, but when he gets home — then the kitchen temperature really rises. Not everyone can be sold on the sweeter form of stuffing, but this one is not *too* sweet, and it definitely does something for wild turkey.

HOW TO COOK

Place ⅛ pound of butter in a saucepan and in it brown 2 diced shallots, then add 1 cup of chopped celery, sauté over a low flame for two minutes, then strain off butter and place shallots and celery in a mixing bowl. To them add 2 tablespoons of chopped parsley, salt and pepper, 1 teaspoon of paprika, ½ teaspoon of marjoram, ¼ teaspoon of rosemary, 2 pinches of ground cloves, 1 cup of crushed pineapple, 2 cups of browned breadcrumbs, and ½ cup of heavy cream. Blend well with wooden spoon, adding sufficient chicken stock to moisten properly, then put aside. To the butter strained from the shallots and celery in the saucepan add the chopped liver, heart and gizzard of the turkey, sauté them over a low flame until tender, then add two cups of chicken stock, bring to a boil, then simmer for 20 minutes. Stuff the turkey with the dressing, sewing opening carefully. Rub the entire turkey thoroughly with the ⅜ pound of butter, and add remainder of butter to the chicken stock. Place the turkey in a shallow roasting pan in an oven preheated to 500 degrees. Cook for 15 minutes, then reduce oven to 350 degrees and roast for 15 minutes to the pound, basting frequently with butter-and-chicken-stock mixture. About ½ hour before turkey is done put liver, heart and gizzard from basting pan into the roasting pan. When turkey is tender, remove to warming oven. Place roasting pan over low flame, add ½ cup of boiling water, then stir and scrape pan until gravy thickens. If necessary add ½ cup of Béchamel sauce as a thickening agent.

Note:

Many prefer to cook only half a wild turkey at one time. The bird should be carefully split "from stem to stern" down the breast and spine. Prepare one third of the stuffing recipes given, turn the turkey skin-side down, and fill the hollow cavity with the stuffing. Care must be taken in placing the bird in the roasting pan. The half turkey should be basted with even more frequency than the whole bird, as it tends to dry out more readily.

This is one of the finest methods of preparing wild turkey, for it seems to preserve *all* of the flavor and retains the juices of the bird, as it seals and sears during the first few turns.

Turkey on the Spit

Any one of the stuffing recipes listed in this chapter can be used, but the bird should be carefully rubbed with butter after being impaled on the spit, and basting should be done with greater frequency. You will need a large drip pan, and when the basting liquor is used up the bird should be basted with the drippings.

First prepare a basting brush, either by wrapping a dozen sprigs of parsley around the end of the short stick, or by tying three or four stalks of leafy celery with string at their base and two thirds of the way up the stalk.

The turkey should be four or five inches from the charcoal basket, and if the bird seems to be browning too soon, it should be moved back another two inches. When done it should be removed to a warm oven immediately.

The following bastings are excellent for wild turkey.

Turkey Bastings

Basting #1

HOW TO PREPARE

Place all of the ingredients with the exception of the butter in a saucepan and simmer for ten minutes over a low flame with a lid on the pan. Remove from fire, stir in the butter.

Requirements
1 cup of rosé wine
½ teaspoon of rosemary
¼ teaspoon of chervil
1 pinch of ginger
½ teaspoon of salt
1 tablespoon of lemon juice
⅙ pound of butter

Basting #2

HOW TO PREPARE

Place all of the ingredients other than the butter in a saucepan and simmer for five minutes, then add the butter and stir in until melted.

Requirements
1 cup of orange juice
2 tablespoons of lemon juice
3 tablespoons of Cointreau
½ teaspoon of basil
¼ teaspoon of tarragon
¼ pound of butter

Requirements
1 cup of orange juice
½ cup of lemon juice
¼ teaspoon of rosemary
1 cup of dry white wine
½ cup of butter

Piquant

HOW TO PREPARE

Melt the butter in a saucepan, add the other ingredients, bring to a low simmer for two minutes. Remove from heat. (Some prefer steeping the rosemary in the wine for five minutes before adding it.)

Requirements
1 cup of sweet cider
2 ounces of applejack
1 cup of Graves (sauterne)
½ cup of butter
¼ teaspoon of tarragon

Cider-Wine

HOW TO PREPARE

Place all ingredients in a saucepan and bring to a boil, then simmer for five minutes. Remove from heat.

7
Venison
(Deer, Elk, Moose, Caribou)

VENISON, like other forms of game, is favored by the gourmet not because it happens to be rare, and in many instances extremely difficult to obtain, but because of its exceptional flavor. Despite this, or perhaps because of it, a large percentage of American cooks (including some professionals) prepare this meat in a manner that destroys not only its flavor but its texture. Probably no other item of game so suffers from improper, or possibly *ill-advised,* preparations as does venison.

There is a simple rule that may be followed in the preparation of venison — cook it as you would beef. Not like pork, mutton, lamb or veal, but like beef. This applies, of course, only to those who prepare beef in a manner that insures the retention of its natural juices. For those who prefer their steaks, fillets and roasts well done, I have a request to make. Please skip over this entire section. Such gustatory outlaws will find nothing of interest in these pages.

Overcooking is more destructive to the flavor and texture of venison than it is to beef, for venison (except for the rare moose) does not have the layers and striations of fat as does beef, therefore it tends to dry out more quickly and thoroughly under the application of heat. The flavor evaporates and the fibers become tough and hard.

In the proper preparation of venison, the larding needle is a *must*. Occasionally you find venison that has an exterior larding or coating of fat. This does not mean that you can ignore the larding needle, it merely means that the chances are you have been fortunate enough to obtain a tender, juicy bit of meat. In my own preparation of venison I remove *all* the fatty tissue I find, for once cooked, the resultant fat is a tallowlike substance that is both repulsive and tasteless. For this I substitute beef fat or salt pork.

Venison roasts cannot be popped into the oven and ignored, while the cook joins his guest in the pleasant task of sopping up cocktails. It is necessary to baste such roasts frequently, for a hot oven rather than a warm, slow oven is vital to the proper preparation of this meat. Also, the initial searing of the meat is important. I have known some meticulous cooks who first sear the roast on all sides in a hot broiler before removing it to the oven.

Venison has one other thing in common with beef — proper curing. The hunter must dress, clean and cool his deer as soon as possible, and hang it to air after making certain no fly can get at it. Failure to do this will sour the meat. Upon returning home the hunter should arrange to have the meat hung in a "curing room" (usually the local butcher will cooperate) for not less than three weeks. Personally, I prefer to skin the deer before curing it, although not everyone agrees with this procedure. Once it has been properly cured it can be butchered and packaged for the freezer. Meat that goes into the freezer improperly cured will emerge from the freezer exactly as it went in. A stout oil-paper wrapper, followed by an airtight plastic bag, is the only sound preparation for freezing. If the venison is exposed to air in the deep-freeze it will dry out in two months.

It is also important to insure that the individual frozen "cuts" are of the proper size. Too many put venison away in individual bags that, when thawed out, provide more meat than is wanted.

I know a few individuals who, before storing their venison, prepare it for immediate cooking. That is, they do the larding and "blanketing" of roasts, and the "stripping" of chops, before wrapping it for the freezer. My own preference is to carry out these tasks after the meat has been removed from the freezer and thawed out.

For those willing to devote a reasonable amount of time to the preparation of venison, the reward is great.

Fritz Pruyn, whose Adirondack hunting lodge is fitted with unusually complete culinary apparatus, is one of the most dedicated and able amateur chefs I have ever encountered. The time he spends in the big kitchen cuts deeply into his hunting time, but he does not seem to mind, and his guests benefit as a result of his sacrifice. In common with many interested cooks, he glares, curses and hovers on the fringe of temper if his guests are not waiting when the food is ready. And who can point a finger at this attitude? If he is willing to do the work, his guests should be willing to be punctual.

My first sample of his skill was fortunate, for of all cuts I consider the saddle to be the peak in texture and flavor. Fritz "saws," not "chops," the ribs off close to the fillet, and the ribs promptly go into his "stock pot" which always seems to be simmering on the back of the big range.

HOW TO COOK

With the larding needle run a ¼-inch strip of salt pork through each fillet, about ½ inch from the top. Slice two cloves of garlic into toothpick-thin slivers, and insert at intervals along both fillets, puncturing the holes for the garlic with an awl. Slice the remainder of the salt pork into very thin strips and cover the fillets. Place in a shallow roasting pan (rib ends down) and put in an oven that has been preheated to the maximum (normally 550 degrees) for five minutes. Reduce the oven to 450 degrees and baste thoroughly with drippings. Continue to baste every eight to ten minutes for 1½ hours. Remove from oven, place saddle in another pan and return to oven after extinguishing the flame (or put in warming oven if available). Place roasting pan on top of stove over low flame and stir 2 tablespoons of flour into the drippings, scraping bottom of pan in process. Add 4 ounces of dry red wine, salt and pepper to taste, and stir until gravy has thickened.

Note

In carving venison saddle, make the cut with a sharp knife *lengthwise*, not across, the fillet, making slices about ¼-inch thick. Properly prepared, the meat is well browned outside and bright pink inside, and as tender and juicy as anyone could ask. With merged mashed potatoes and white turnips (whipped with an egg beater), broccoli with hollandaise sauce, and a tossed green salad, you will agree that there could not possibly be a finer repast. Of course, you might add a bottle of good claret.

Pruyn Venison Saddle

Requirements
1 saddle of venison
    (full length of fillet)
¼ pound of fat salt pork
2 cloves of garlic
4 ounces of dry red wine
2 tablespoons of flour
salt
freshly ground
    black pepper

Venison Fillet à la Dupont

Requirements

8 one-inch-thick slices of fillet
¼ pound of butter
2 tomatoes
1 tablespoon of parsley
2 tablespoons of grated onion
salt
freshly ground black pepper
1 cup of diced button mushrooms

In his small Wisconsin duck-shooting camp, Augustin Dupont has two very small, Spartan bedrooms and one very large kitchen. The afternoon the four of us arrived was cold, blustery and an occasional spatter of sleet promised traditional duck-hunting weather. While the three guests walked down to the shore of the lake and looked over the precincts, Gus was stoking the range and sorting out his food parcels. Upon our return, greeted with a welcome mug of hot buttered rum, Gus informed us that the dinner that night would be a variation from routine. "Tonight we spread. The rest of the week we eat ducks." As all of us liked ducks, this did not seem too ominous a portent, but we were rather eager for the "spread." It had been a long time between meals.

While the others continued with the hot buttered rum, I sneaked down to the range end of the room, and was rather puzzled to see Gus light the (bottled) gas broiler to get it "hotted up" as he explained it. Big Idaho potatoes had gone into the oven of the range some time before, and Gus was now busy with the important preparations. Removing a long, heavy package from the refrigerator, Gus revealed two nice venison fillets. "I've had these in the freezer since last winter," he explained, "and it's time they came out to make room for this year's venison."

An hour later we had the "spread" and it *was* a spread.

HOW TO COOK

Place the eight fillets in a shallow pan, first rubbing them thoroughly with softened butter until they have a film of butter. Place (close to flame) under a *very* hot broiler for exactly five minutes. Remove from broiler and turn each fillet. Cap each fillet with one slice of tomato, ¼ tablespoon of grated onion on tomato, and sprinkle each with minced parsley. Salt and pepper to taste. Replace in broiler about 1½ inches from flame and broil for another five minutes. Remove fillets to hot platter and put in warming oven. Place pan over light flame and sauté one cup of diced button mushrooms in butter drippings. Pour over fillets and serve. With mealy Idahos with plenty of butter, garlic bread, julienne string beans and a hearts of lettuce salad, it was a real "spread." With it we had cold, pale ale.

A few years ago I was fortunate enough to be invited for ten days of shooting at Bluhnbach, the amazing hunting lodge of Alfried Krupp in the heart of the Austrian Alps. The hunting was superb and the food, because of a wealth of game coupled with culinary art, was — well, a gourmet would have stowed away in the huge old castle. I came away with a number of choice recipes, involving various forms of venison, obtained from *Hirsch,* rebok and chamois. I will simplify the names of these recipes, for the combined Austrian-French-German terms are somewhat involved.

Venison Bluhnbach

HOW TO COOK

With an awl or ice pick, insert thin slivers of garlic (two cloves) in the fillet. In an earthenware crock prepare the following marinade: one pint of red wine, one cup of water, 4 peppercorns, two bay leaves, two tablespoons of tarragon, 1 tablespoon of salt, 1 level teaspoon of freshly ground black pepper. Stir thoroughly and then place fillet in marinade in a cool place (not refrigerator) for 24 hours, turning three or four times and making certain it is covered by marinade. Remove from marinade, place in a shallow roasting pan and cover with thin slices of salt pork. Place in an oven preheated to 450 degrees and roast for 2 to 2½ hours, basting frequently with drippings. Remove from oven, remove salt pork, and place fillet on a platter and in warming oven. Pour off half of the drippings, place roasting pan over a light flame and add 1 cup of strained marinade and 1 wineglass of Calvados. Stir briskly and slowly add two cups of sour cream. Pour over fillet on platter and serve. Carve in slices, across the grain, ½-inch thick.

Fillet Marinade Bluhnbach

Requirements

1 eight-to ten-pound
    venison fillet
    (or equivalent)
1 pint of dry red wine
1 wineglass Calvados
    (or applejack)
4 peppercorns
2 tablespoons of tarragon
2 cloves of garlic
2 bay leaves
½ pound of fat salt pork
2 cups of sour cream
salt
freshly ground
    black pepper

Venison Paprika Bluhnbach

Requirements

3 pounds of venison steak
⅙ pound of butter
4 medium onions
    (size of a golf ball)
2 cloves of garlic
1 teaspoon marjoram
1 cup diced tomatoes
1 wineglass of dry sherry
2 tablespoons of paprika
1 cup of sour cream
½ cup of flour
salt
freshly ground
    black pepper

HOW TO COOK

Cut steak into one-inch cubes. In a brown-paper bag place ½ cup of flour, salt and pepper. Shake up cubes of steak until dusted. In a large skillet melt one-sixth pound of butter. When hot, add cubes of steak and lightly brown them. Remove steak and to pan add four medium onions diced fine, two cloves of garlic minced, 1 teaspoon of marjoram, 1 cup of diced tomatoes, 1 wineglass of dry sherry, 2 tablespoons of paprika, and cook slowly, with lid on the skillet, for fifteen minutes. Add the cube steak, replace lid on skillet and cook slowly until steak is tender (45 minutes to 1 hour). Stir in one cup of sour cream and serve.

Venison Hunter Style, Bluhnbach

Requirements

4 pounds of venison
6 small carrots
6 small onions
½ cup of flour
1 tablespoon of tarragon
½ teaspoon powdered dill
4 stalks of celery
½ cup chopped parsley
1 pint of dry white wine
1 cup of beef stock
    (or consommé)
2 bay leaves
6 peppercorns
2 tablespoons of paprika
salt
freshly ground
    black pepper
⅙ pound butter

HOW TO COOK

Cut four pounds of venison into 2-inch sections. In a brown-paper bag place ½ cup of flour, salt and pepper. Drop in venison sections and shake bag until sections are well dusted with flour. In a large skillet melt ⅙ pound of butter and when hot, sauté the venison sections until lightly browned. Arrange browned venison sections in a large earthenware casserole and add the following: 6 small carrots cut in half lengthwise, six onions chopped, 1 tablespoon of tarragon (rubbed to powder), ½ teaspoon of powdered dill, four stalks of celery (chopped fine, leaves included), ½ cup of chopped parsley, 6 peppercorns, 2 bay leaves, 2 tablespoons of paprika, 1 cup of beef stock, 1 pint of dry white wine. Cover the casserole and place in a 325-degree oven for 1½ hours. In the butter remaining in the skillet, brown 2 tablespoons of flour, and add only enough water to make a smooth paste. Remove the venison sections from the casserole and force the stock and vegetables through a medium sieve, then return the venison to the casserole and keep warm. Add the strained stock to the skillet, stirring constantly over a low flame until it thickens, then pour over venison sections in casserole. Return casserole to oven for 15 minutes, then remove and serve. The venison will be tender but not dry.

HOW TO COOK

With ¼ pound of salt pork cut into ¼-inch strips, use larding needle to thoroughly lard the haunch. In a large earthenware crock prepare the following marinade — one quart of dry red wine, 3 large onions sliced thin, 3 bay leaves, 1 crushed clove of garlic, ½ cup of lemon juice, salt and pepper, 4 crushed peppercorns, 4 cloves, ½ teaspoon of ginger, ½ teaspoon of powdered dill, 1 teaspoon of tarragon, 1 teaspoon of basil. (It is preferable to bring this marinade to a boil in a kettle, then cool, before placing in crock.) Marinate the haunch of venison in the crock for eight to ten hours, turning at least four times. After marinating, dry the haunch thoroughly, then cut two cloves of garlic into thin slivers and insert in the haunch by punching holes with awl or ice pick. Place haunch in a shallow roasting pan and cover with thinly sliced (¼ pound) salt pork. Meanwhile, place marinade in an open saucepan over brisk flame and reduce by half, then strain. Place haunch in an oven preheated to 450 degrees. Baste frequently with drippings and marinade. It should roast for 20 minutes to the pound. When tender, remove from oven, place on platter in warming oven. Place roasting pan over light flame. Make a paste of 3 tablespoons of flour and remaining marinade and stir into drippings until thickened. Then add one cup of red or black currant jelly, stirring briskly until merged. Remove haunch from warming oven and serve with the gravy.

Roast Haunch of Venison, Bluhnbach

Requirements

1 ten- to twelve-pound
    haunch of venison
1 quart of dry red wine
3 large onions
3 bay leaves
3 cloves of garlic
3 tablespoons of flour
½ pound fat salt pork
½ cup of lemon juice
4 cloves
½ teaspoon of ginger
    (powdered)
½ teaspoon powdered dill
1 teaspoon of tarragon
1 teaspoon of basil
1 cup of red or black
    currant jelly
salt
freshly ground
    black pepper
4 peppercorns

Spitted Roast of Venison, Bluhnbach

Requirements

1 10-pound roast
    of venison
3 cloves of garlic
½ pound of salt pork
1 pint of dry red wine
1 large onion
1 tablespoon of rosemary
½ cup of lemon juice
1 wineglass of cognac
6 cloves
6 peppercorns
salt
freshly ground
    black pepper
1 dozen sprigs of parsley

The spit at Bluhnbach is the same, in design, as the one used in that very kitchen on the same hearth, eight hundred years ago. It is not at all beyond the realm of possibility that an ancestor of the kitchen boy once had the same tiresome task in *his* youth. The modern spit, turned by a clockwork mechanism or a small electric motor, is little different in principle, and the method of cooking is the same.

HOW TO COOK

First place in a saucepan 1 pint of dry red wine, one large onion sliced thin, 1 crushed clove of garlic, ½ cup of lemon juice, 6 cloves, 6 peppercorns (crushed), 1 teaspoon of salt, pepper, and one tablespoon of rosemary. Place over a brisk flame and boil for ten minutes. While this is boiling, cut ½ pound of fat salt pork into strips 5 inches long and ¼-inch in diameter. With a larding needle work these strips in and out of the roast, penetrating about ½ inch and leaving one inch of each end of the strip protruding. Cut two cloves of garlic into thin slivers and insert with an awl or ice pick into the roast. Place the roast on the spit and adjust the drip pan so the drippings fall into it. Strain the wine and stock from the saucepan and place in a handy receptacle. Form a brush at the end of a stick with a dozen sprigs of parsley, by wrapping the stems around the stick and tying with string. Using this brush, apply the stock as a basting to the roast. Eventually the salt pork drippings will merge with the stock. The roast should be basted at least once every other complete turn. Continue basting until the roast is tender. At Bluhnbach this was served with creamed parsnips, large green beans, hot herb rolls and a green salad.

Venison Cutlet Forester Style, Bluhnbach

Requirements

2 pounds of venison cutlets
½ pound of salt pork
1½ cups of breadcrumbs
2 eggs
1 cup of milk
1 tablespoon of powdered
    dill
2 lemons
salt
freshly ground black pepper

HOW TO COOK

Cut two pounds of venison steaks about ½ inch thick and pound lightly on a hard surface with a wooden mallet until about ¼ inch thick. Sprinkle both sides of the cutlets with powdered dill, rubbing it into the meat, then salt and pepper each cutlet, also rubbing it in. Beat two eggs and one cup of milk and pour into a flat pan. Into another flat pan spread 1½ cups of crisp breadcrumbs. Dip cutlets into the egg-milk and then in the breadcrumbs until both sides are breaded. Put to one side on waxed paper. Into a large skillet place ½ pound of salt pork sliced thin. Render the fat from the salt pork, then remove the crisp pork. Fry the cutlets in the hot pork fat, then place on brown paper to drain. Serve with a lemon slice. (The crisp salt pork slices were crumbled into tiny bits and added to the tossed salad.)

There are still a few lone gold prospectors in Alaska, and Bob Hammond is one of them, although he ekes out his income with a bit of trapping and agate-collecting on the side. Bob lives in a fairly large, warm, tight and extremely comfortable one-room cabin where a small river empties into a large lake on the Alaskan peninsula. He keeps a large stock of assorted whiskies and never touches a drop, which was something of a mystery until he explained. Bush pilots often drop in for the night. Here they know they will get a warming drink and a good meal. In return Hammond gets company and an assortment of newspapers and magazines. One hand, in brief, washes the other. Although he is rather limited as to the variety of meat, Hammond compensates by preparing it in varied ways, and is an extremely competent and discriminating cook. The first meal I had there was a form of venison cassoulet, which he termed Venison con Beans. He explains this as follows. "My pleasures are rather simple ones, as you can understand. I went to San Antonio once, and had something they called Chile con Carne, which seemed to be mostly beef and beans. I now have what I call Venison con Beans, just to complicate things. I love to complicate things, but I damn seldom get a chance." Anyway, it was delicious.

Venison con Beans, Hammond

Requirements
2 pounds of venison
1 quart of white
　　dried beans
1 bay leaf
4 large onions
½ pound of salt pork
3 tablespoons of
　　Worcestershire sauce
2 carrots (when
　　he had them)
1 teaspoon oregano
　　(he always had)
1 bottle of beer (when
　　he could spare it)
salt
black pepper

HOW TO COOK

Soak one quart of beans overnight in salted water. Drain the beans and place them in an earthenware casserole with the following: one bottle of beer, 1 bay leaf, ½ pound of salt pork cut in one-inch cubes, 2 carrots diced, 4 large onions, sliced thin, 1 bay leaf, 3 tablespoons of Worcestershire sauce, 1 teaspoon of oregano, salt and pepper. Place the cover on the casserole and put in a 350-degree oven for five to six hours. Remove the cover and add two pounds of venison cut in one-inch cubes, stir carefully into beans, replace cover, and return to 350-degree oven for another two hours. This is a "one-pot" meal, and with sourdough biscuits, a gallon of hot, strong tea and a slug of fine old bourbon (that's what it said on the bottle) you find yourself replete and happy.

Venison Steak Exotic

Requirements
2 large venison steaks
1 tablespoon of
    parsley (chopped)
1 tablespoon
    Worcestershire sauce
2 ounces of
    Roquefort cheese
1 medium onion
¼ teaspoon Tabasco sauce
1 tablespoon of lemon juice
salt
pepper
⅛ pound of butter

This dish undoubtedly originated in France, Spain or Portugal, but I encountered it about fifty miles southwest of San Antonio, as the buzzard flies, which was something of a surprise to everyone concerned. For three days I had been eating beef in varied forms, mostly in the form of thick steaks, although with a liberal sprinkling of Spanish or, rather, Mexican interpretations. Unfortunately, and unfairly, I cannot recall the name of my host at that particular meal, as I was the guest of an enthusiastic Texan who was going to show me some real turkey shooting if it killed all of us. We moved from ranch to ranch, and eventually encountered a rancher with a penchant for the exotic. He called it Lone Star Venison Steak, which was, I believe, a patriotic gesture. My host for the trip had more imagination and a better vocabulary, so he called it Exotic.

HOW TO COOK

The sauce is prepared in advance. Blend the following ingredients in a bowl — 2 ounces of Roquefort cheese, 1 tablespoon of chopped parsley, 1 tablespoon of Worcestershire sauce, ¼ teaspoon of Tabasco sauce, 1 tablespoon of lemon juice, 1 grated onion. Mix thoroughly with a wooden spoon until a firm paste results. Rub two 1½-inch-thick venison steaks with butter and broil rapidly under a hot flame. When the steaks are almost done, remove them from broiler and coat one surface of each with the prepared paste. Return them to the broiler for half a minute, two inches from the flame, and serve. I have tried this since on elk and moose. Delicious!

There is a small inn above the Rauma in Norway, near Troll-stegen that should be avoided at all costs by any visitor who is worried about his (or her) waistline. According to the host, the food is no different than that found in any of the small inns, although he admits that unusual attention is given to the preparation. In cutting up a deer, there are certain portions that must be allocated to one or two forms of preparation — stew or "hamburger." Venisonburger, if you wish. The old-timer, of course, stores some of these bits and pieces away for mince pie, for venison makes incomparable mincemeat. At the inn, they served this hamburger in an unusual form, and I pestered the host until I obtained the recipe. Prior to the sausage, of course, we went through a half-dozen fish courses, the basis for which primarily involved herrings and salmon. All courses were accompanied by ice-cold aquavit.

HOW TO COOK

Grind 2 pounds of venison and one pound of very fat pork at the same time, and insure that the two meats are combined thoroughly. In a skillet melt ⅛ pound of butter and add one chopped onion. Sauté onion slowly for ten minutes. Soak 1 cup of breadcrumbs in 1½ cups of light cream. To the vension-pork burger add the onions with the butter, the cream and bread-crumbs, ¾ teaspoon of pepper, 1½ teaspoons of salt, 2 eggs beaten, 2 tablespoons of chopped parsley, ⅛ teaspoon of sage, ⅛ teaspoon of basil, and merge all these ingredients thoroughly. Now melt ⅛ pound of butter in the same skillet, form the sausage into balls about 1½ inches in diameter, and sauté them in butter until brown, adding a bit more butter if necessary. Remove the sausage balls to a warming oven. Add 1 tablespoon of flour to the skillet and stir until browned. Slowly stir in 1½ cups of heavy cream (or sour cream) and check the seasoning. Pour this gravy over the sausage balls and serve. After trying it you may decide to sacrifice a "good" cut of venison occasionally just to duplicate the dish. It is especially good for a buffet supper, accompanied by wild rice, green beans, herb rolls and a green salad.

Trollstegen Venison Sausage

Requirements
2 pounds of ground
    venison (ground twice)
1 pound of fat pork
¼ pound of butter
1 medium-sized onion
2 eggs
2 tablespoons of
    chopped parsley
1 cup of light cream
⅛ teaspoon of sage
⅛ teaspoon of basil
1 tablespoon of flour
1 cup of breadcrumbs
1½ cups of heavy cream
    (sour cream is
    satisfactory)
¾ teaspoon of freshly
    ground black pepper
1¼ teaspoons of salt

Venison Pot Roast Russell

Requirements

8 pound venison roast
¼ pound salt pork
⅛ pound of butter
3 medium onions
2 bay leaves
¼ teaspoon of allspice
4 tablespoons of honey
4 fillets of anchovy
2 tablespoons of vinegar
2 tablespoons of flour
2 cups of heavy cream
    (or sour cream)
salt
freshly ground
    black pepper
3 large carrots
1 clove of garlic
1 wineglass of cognac

Bob Russell, mentioned in other parts of this volume, who prefers his meat *rare* and preferably broiled, considers venison to be one of the finest forms of edible flesh available, which caused me to recoil when he announced that venison pot roast was on the menu at the hunting shack. "The best of us, along with the worst of us — and I shall refuse to state my category — occasionally runs up against a bit of venison that derived from — shall we say — an elderly buck. I gathered in a real grandfather last month. He had a magnificent rack of antlers, but the meat! The guide warned me that I'd be unable to push a fork in the gravy. So, pot roast, here we come."

Knowing Bob I had an idea it would be an unusual pot roast, and it was.

HOW TO COOK

Rub the roast thoroughly with salt and pepper after having run six ¼-inch strips of salt pork through the meat (end to end) with a larding needle. (I have found the back fat of beef preferable to salt pork for this larding.) In a large iron pot (with a lid) melt ⅛ pound of butter and when it is hot add the roast, turning it frequently until it is browned. Add 3 medium onions chopped fine, 2 bay leaves, one crushed clove of garlic, 3 carrots quartered lengthwise, 2½ cups of hot water, ¼ teaspoon of allspice, 4 tablespoons of honey, four anchovies (mashed in a cup to which two tablespoons of vinegar have been added), salt, freshly ground black pepper. Stir the liquids thoroughly and bring to a boil, then reduce the heat to a simmer, and cook for 2 to 2½ hours. Remove the roast to a warming oven. Strain the stock and return to the pot, then stir in the heavy cream into which two tablespoons of flour have been blended. Check the seasoning, bring to a boil, and return the roast to this gravy and simmer for five minutes. Stir in one wineglass of cognac and serve.

This is another contribution from the secret file of Bob Russell, and was utilized as a means of disposing of another portion of the "tough buck." He insists that it originated in the Scottish Highlands and was the creation of an expatriate Gaul who was fed up with Napoleon. History relates that a number of highborn Scots were included in Napoleon's officer corps, but a Napoleonic Frenchman in Scotland is a new twist. The dish, however, has a faint Scots-French flavor, if such a combination is within the realm of possiblity.

HOW TO COOK

Cut 3 pounds of venison into one-inch cubes. In a paper bag place ½ cup of flour, 1 teaspoon of salt and ¼ teaspoon of pepper. Place the cubed venison in the bag and shake well until all cubes are well dusted with flour. In a skillet place ⅙ pound of butter and over a medium flame brown the cubed vension. In an earthenware pot place 8 leeks cut in 2-inch sections, 1 minced clove of garlic, 1 cup of beef stock, 1 teaspoon of basil, salt and pepper to taste. Place a lid on the pot and put in 350-degree oven for one hour. At this time put a low flame under the skillet and add one wineglass of dry sherry to the butter and cubed venison, then gradually stir in ½ cup of heavy cream, not permitting it to boil. Remove the earthenware pot from the oven, add the contents of the skillet, stir carefully, replace the cover and return the pot to the oven for another hour, retaining the same temperature, 350 degrees. Bob served this with white rice, green limas, and a hearts of lettuce salad with Roquefort cheese dressing.

Venison with Leeks

Requirements
3 pounds of venison
⅙ pound of butter
8 leeks
1 cup of beef stock
    (or consommé)
½ cup of heavy cream
½ cup of flour
1 clove of garlic
1 teaspoon of basil
1 wineglass of dry sherry
salt
freshly ground
    black pepper

Venison Scallopini

Requirements

4 half-inch venison steaks
½ cup of finely grated
    Parmesan cheese
4 tablespoons of olive oil
1 clove of garlic
2 lemons
2 wineglasses of Marsala
⅔ cup of beef consommé
½ teaspoon basil
½ teaspoon of oregano
salt
freshly ground
    black pepper

It would be a practical impossibility to find an Italian restaurant anywhere in the world (where a calf could be found) that did not serve veal scallopini. It is a dish that lends itself admirably to veal, and, you will discover, even more admirably to venison. Michael Novelli, who usually locates an unsuspecting deer while roaming the hills of northern Vermont, has converted an old stone farmhouse not far from Lake Champlain into a comfortable hunting lodge. When you enter the big kitchen at the end of a hard day in the hills, you could close your eyes and open them again with the conviction that you were in another kitchen on the slopes of Monte Rumichi, in Mike's beloved Apennines. Each year he sends a truck to a certain valley in upstate New York and it returns with a load of grapes. In the fullness of time Mike transmutes these purple globes into a full-bodied dry wine, which he uses in his cooking and for the pleasant task of washing down in his fine food. Venison Scallopini is one of his favorite dishes.

HOW TO COOK

Pound 4 half-inch venison steaks with a wooden mallet until they are ¼ inch thick. Place each steak on a wooden surface, sprinkle with Parmesan cheese and tap lightly with the mallet until the cheese is worked into the meat. Do the same on the reverse side. Lightly salt and pepper, then cut the meat into two-by-four-inch sections. In a large skillet heat 4 tablespoons of olive oil and place a crushed clove of garlic in it, stirring it around until well browned. Remove the garlic and dispose of it. Place the strips of venison in the skillet and lightly brown them on both sides. Add ⅔ of a cup of beef stock, 2 wineglasses of Marsala, ½ teaspoon of basil, ½ teaspoon of oregano (rubbed to dust) and 4 tablespoons of lemon juice. Place a cover on the skillet and simmer lightly for twenty minutes. Remove to a hot platter and place a paper-thin slice of lemon on each cutlet. Mike serves this with green noodles, hot garlic bread, baked squash, tossed salad with a sharp dressing, and pitchers of his own Chianti. Mike, incidentally, bakes the long, slender loaves of Italian bread himself, using equal parts of white, whole wheat and rye flour. Lunch, when you hunt with Mike, is this crusty, delicious bread, butter, cheese, large red onions, and gallons of strong tea. The tea shows a north-woods influence. It would float a cartridge.

When Dr. Albert Simard wants to give a few friends a snack, he is willing to take the time and effort to make it a good one. Fortunately for him, his New York hideout is adjacent to shops where assorted delicacies from all corners of the world are available. As his refrigerator always seems to have an adequate supply of assorted sauces in sealed jars, he seems able to whip up what appears to be a complicated dish in a very short time. Some of the sauces favored by him, as well as by other *gentilhommes chefs de cuisine,* will be listed in the back of this volume.

HOW TO COOK

Melt ⅙ pound of butter in a skillet over a hot flame. When butter "sizzles," sauté 4 one-inch venison fillets for 3 to 4 minutes on each side. Remove the fillets and place them in a warming oven. To the remaining butter in the skillet add 1 wineglass of Madeira, ½ cup of Espagnol sauce, 2 tablespoons of chopped truffles, four large mushroom caps, ⅓ teaspoon of salt, pepper to taste. Simmer slowly over moderate flame for six minutes. Meanwhile, prepare 4 half-inch slices of lightly toasted bread, and spread them with the contents of a 2-ounce can of *pâté de foie gras.* Place the "tournedos" on the toast, top each with a mushroom cap, and spoon the sauce over all. This, in my opinion, is the snack to end all snacks, and a glass or even two glasses of lightly chilled Tavel puts just the righ touch to it.

Bob Russell, not to be outdone, prepares an almost similar dish. He broils the fillets, and eliminates the truffles and mushroom caps, substituting chopped button mushrooms. It is *almost* as good, although I would hate for Bob to hear me make this admission.

Venison Tournedos

Requirements
4 one-inch thick slices of
    venison fillet
⅙ pound of butter
1 wineglass of Madeira
½ cup of Espagnol sauce
2 tablespoons of chopped
    truffles
4 large mushroom caps
2 ounce can of
    pâté de foie gras
salt
pepper

Venison Patties Oregon

Requirements

2 pounds of venison
½ pound of salt pork
⅛ pound of butter
2 cups of finely chopped
    green onions (scallions)
1 ½ teaspoons fresh
    horseradish
    (3 teaspoons prepared
    horseradish)
1 tablespoon
    Worcestershire sauce
1 dash of Tabasco sauce
salt
black pepper
½ teaspoon of dry mustard

Gene Brighton, who sells insurance and insists that he lives, works and enjoys life "all over Oregon," but prefers a rough log shack on the margin of the Alsea River, is a better-than-average amateur chef. He insists that his Venison Patties Oregon was his own, and his alone, invention, discovery and concoction. "I came up with it after a long period of mediation and experimentation," he insists, "and it provides a magnificent end for such scraps, slivers and bits of meat as are ill-suited for stew or broiler." Anyway, here it is.

HOW TO COOK

Put two pounds of venison and ½ pound of (washed) salt pork through the meat grinder twice. Blend venison and pork thoroughly and work in 1 teaspoon of salt and ¼ teaspoon of black pepper. Shape into patties ½ inch thick and 4 inches in diameter and place on waxed paper. In a skillet melt ⅛ pound of butter over a moderate flame, add 2 cups of finely chopped green onions, 1 ½ teaspoons of fresh horseradish (or equivalent), 1 dash of Tabasco sauce, ½ teaspoon of dry mustard and 1 tablespoon of Worcestershire sauce. Stir until ingredients are blended and cook until onions are tender. Spread this over every other meat patty, then cover with adjoining patty and press edges together. Place the patty sandwiches on a shallow roasting pan and slide under pre-heated broiler, 1 ½ to 2 inches from flame. Broil for about six minutes on each side and serve on toasted buttered rolls.

This is a specialty of the Essenerhof, and is an unusual and very delicious method of preparing the fillets of the *Hirsch,* which is a large deer found in Germany and Austria. Had I known the ingredients before ordering this dish, I would have ordered something else, which would have resulted in a definite loss, for I enjoyed it on two subsequent occasions. I have prepared it myself on a number of occasions, trying it with fresh and canned pineapple, and I am satisfied that it is well worth the effort involved in getting the fresh fruit.

HOW TO COOK

Melt two tablespoons of butter in a saucepan, add ½ a peeled pineapple (cut in strips ½ inch thick, 1 inch wide, 2 inches long), and 1 cup of sour pie cherries, and sauté until the fruit glazes, which should take from 15 to 20 minutes over a low flame. In another saucepan place 1 minced shallot, 2 pinches of allspice, ¼ teaspoon of salt, freshly ground black pepper, 1 cup of milk and 1 cup of light cream. Bring to a boil, reduce heat, and simmer for 5 minutes, stirring constantly, then add one cup of fine breadcrumbs, stirring constantly, then add the glazed fruit, Tokay, and stir over low flame for 3 minutes. In a skillet melt the remainder of the butter and when it is brown and smoking add the venison fillets, sautéing them about 3 minutes on each side. Remove the fillets to a hot platter, pour the sauce over them, and serve. You will enjoy every succulent bite.

Sautéed Fillets Essenerhof

Requirements
4 to 6 inch-thick venison
    fillets
½ of a fresh pineapple
1 cup of sour pie cherries
1 wineglass of Tokay (port
    can be substituted)
2 pinches of allspice
1 shallot
1 cup of fine breadcrumbs
salt
freshly ground
    black pepper
¼ pound of butter
1 cup of light cream and
    1 cup of milk

Stuffed Shoulder of Venison

This recipe, according to its sponsor, Calvin Blake, came from the northern tip of Idaho, where you also need a Montana and a Washington license just in case you wander across a state line. I received it in exchange for a recipe I ran in my column many years ago, I tried it, and found it good.

Requirements

1 shoulder of venison
¼ pound of fat salt pork
2 cloves of garlic
1 cup of olive oil
3 cups of browned
    breadcrumbs
1 wineglass of dry sherry
2 small onions
1 teaspoon of rosemary
½ teaspoon of chervil
1 cup of diced apple
1 cup of burgundy
1 pinch of thyme
2 tablespoons of butter
½ cup of beef stock
salt
pepper

HOW TO COOK

Have your butcher (if *you* can't) bone and cut a pocket in a shoulder of venison. In a saucepan melt 2 tablespoons of butter, brown two small onions diced, add ½ teaspoon of rosemary, 1 cup of diced apple, 1 pinch of thyme, then stir in 3 cups of breadcrumbs. Remove from stove and add 1 wineglass of dry sherry and ½ cup of beef stock. In a small skillet render the fat from ¼ pound of fat salt pork cut in ½-inch cubes. Place browned cubes on brown paper until cool, then mix in the stuffing, adding salt and pepper to taste. Rub the inside of the shoulder pocket with salt and pepper, then stuff, sewing up pocket with butcher's twine. Rub outside of shoulder with salt and pepper, puncture sufficiently to insert thin slivers of garlic, rub with olive oil and dust with ½ teaspoon of rosemary and ½ teaspoon of chervil. Wrap tightly in wax paper and put to one side for four hours. When ready for roasting, place in a shallow roasting pan and put in a 450-degree oven for 15 minutes. Reduce heat to 350 degrees and roast for 1½ hours, basting very frequently with a mixture of ½ cup of olive oil and 1 cup of Burgundy. When basting is gone, baste with the drippings. Remove shoulder to a warming oven, place roasting pan on top of stove over low flame and add ½ cup of hot water, stirring and scraping until gravy forms. Serve gravy separately.

Venison Curry

This is an excellent method of preparing leftover venison, especially if you also happen to like curry. If you have a large roast haunch, and have passed through the "sliced cold" stage, the chances are you will be ready for a hot meal. This is it.

HOW TO COOK

In a small skillet place ⅛ pound of butter, when melted add 3 medium-sized onions diced fine and 1 cup of diced apple. Sauté until onions are tender, remove onions and apple and put to one side. Stir 2 tablespoons of flour into the remaining butter in the skillet and when browned stir in one tablespoon of curry powder, then slowly stir in one cup of heated beef stock and ½ cup of Madeira, stirring constantly, then add 1½ tablespoons of lemon juice and 1 pinch of nutmeg, salt and pepper. Stir over low flame until mixture begins to thicken, then stir in the sautéed onions and apple. When this begins to simmer add two cups of cubed venison, simmer for three minutes, then serve in a nest of cooked white rice, along with some chutney.

Requirements

2 cups of cubed cooked
   venison
3 medium-sized onions
1 cup of diced apple
2 tablespoon of flour
1½ tablespoons of lemon
   juice
1 tablespoon of curry
   powder
⅛ pound of butter
1 cup of beef stock
½ cup of Madeira
1 pinch of nutmeg
salt
pepper

Venison Charcoal Broiled

This should be prepared somewhat similarly to charcoal-broiled beef except that it must have prior larding. For this either cooking oil or olive oil is best. At least an hour before broiling, the meat should be rubbed on both sides with a split clove of garlic. It should then be placed in a shallow pan and have a half-cup of the oil poured over it and rubbed in with the fingers on both sides. It should then remain in the pan with the oil for at least an hour, being turned two or three times. It is important to sear the steak on both sides as quickly as possible. For a steak cut 1½ inch thick, I spread another film of oil on each side immediately after the sides are seared. I prefer a vertical grill (or basket) to the standard horizontal grill for venison. In using a vertical grill, after rubbing with the oil, I pin thin strips of salt pork all around the steak, using toothpicks. With the vertical grill this salt pork provides almost constant basting during the broiling.

Spitted Venison

In spit-broiling venison it is recommended that nothing smaller than a six-pound roast be prepared. The meat should first be boned, and if not a compact roast, it should be rolled and tied with butcher's cord every two inches. At least four quarter-inch salt pork larding strips should be run lengthwise (equally spaced) about a half-inch under the surface. The meat should be at least three inches from the coal basket and it should be basted every two or three minutes. The degree of rareness can be tested by making a slight cut with a sharp knife close to the spit bar. A basting brush is essential. This can be quickly made by binding a half-dozen sprigs of parsley to a small stick, or by binding together three or four stalks of leafy celery. Arrange drip pan so basting is not wasted.

The following bastings are excellent:

Basting #1

1 cup of dry red wine, 2 tablespoons of lemon juice, 1 teaspoon of rosemary, 1 minced clove of garlic, ½ cup of olive oil, 1 teaspoon of salt, ¼ teaspoon of freshly ground black pepper. Place these ingredients in a saucepan, bring to a boil while stirring, simmer for five minutes.

Basting #2

1 cup of Madeira, ½ cup of orange juice, ½ teaspoon of grated orange peel, ½ teaspoon of chervil, ½ teaspoon of basil, one small grated onion, 1 teaspoon of salt, ¼ teaspoon of pepper, ½ cup of olive oil. Place in a saucepan, simmer for five minutes.

Basting #3

1 cup of cider, 1 small grated onion, 1 teaspoon of salt, ¼ teaspoon of black pepper, 2 pinches of powdered ginger, 1 teaspoon of rosemary, ¼ teaspoon of tarragon, 1 tablespoon of minced parsley, ½ cup of fat rendered from salt pork. Place all ingredients except fat in a saucepan and simmer for ten minutes, add fat and remove from heat.

Basting #4

1 cup of tomato juice, 3 tablespoons of lemon juice, ½ teaspoon of grated lemon peel, one medium-sized onion grated fine, 1 teaspoon of prepared mustard, 2 tablespoons of Worcestershire sauce, ¼ teaspoon of Tabasco sauce, 1 ½ teaspoons of salt, 1 teaspoon of tarragon, ½ cup of water, ½ cup of cooking oil. Simmer all ingredients except oil for 15 minutes, stirring frequently. Add the oil and simmer for another two minutes, stirring constantly.

When you cut up your venison for freezer packing, don't ignore the bones. Save the neck and neck meat, shanks, hips and other bony odds and ends, and devote a few freezer packages to these tidbits. They can provide you with stock as well as excellent soup. I have two favorite venison soups, one a clear soup, the other a form of minestrone. One is a fine prelude to any meal, the other can provide a good, solid luncheon.

Venison Soups

HOW TO COOK

In a large kettle place 4 pounds of venison bones, 1 pound of venison stew meat, 2 large onions diced, 4 sprigs of parsley, 4 stalks of celery, 4 peppercorns, 1 bay leaf, 1 tablespoon of salt and 3 quarts of water. Bring to a boil, then reduce to a slow simmer and place lid on kettle. Cook for two hours, remove from stove and allow to cool long enough to skim fat from surface. Strain through a sieve, remove ½ cup of the stew meat and chop into ¼-inch bits. Replace stock and ½ cup of meat in the kettle, add 8-ounce can of ceci beans, ½ cup of diced carrots, ½ cup of leftover string beans (limas or peas), ½ cup of diced celery, and one minced clove of garlic. Bring to a boil, add ½ cup of elbow macaroni, and reduce flame to a simmer. Place lid on kettle and simmer for 1 hour. This soup has *body*.

Venison Pot au Feu

Requirements

4 pounds of venison bones
1 pound of venison stew meat
2 large onions
4 sprigs of parsley
4 stalks of celery
4 peppercorns
1 bay leaf
1 eight-ounce can ceci beans with liquid
½ cup of diced carrots
½ cup of leftover string beans or limas or peas
½ cup of uncooked elbow macaroni
½ cup of diced celery
1 teaspoon of salt
1 clove of garlic

Clear Venison Soup

Requirements
About 3 pounds of venison
    bones
1 pound of scrap venison
4 stalks of celery (including
    tops)
2 onions
1 clove of garlic
2 carrots
4 sprigs of parsley
2 peppercorns
1 teaspoon of salt
grated Parmesan cheese

HOW TO COOK

In a large kettle place 3 pounds of venison bones and 1 pound of scrap venison (bits of meat ranging in size from an inch to four or five inches), 4 stalks of celery, 2 minced onions, 1 minced clove of garlic, 2 diced carrots, 4 sprigs of parsley, 2 peppercorns, 1 teaspoon of salt and 3 quarts of water. Bring to a boil then reduce to a simmer, place a lid on the kettle, and reduce the liquid to 1 quart. This should take from 2 to 2½ hours. Skim the fat from the top, strain through a sieve, then through cheesecloth, and place in the refrigerator. When it has cooled, skim the remainder of the fat from the top and it is ready to serve at any time. A half-hour before serving cut the crusts from three slices of bread cut a half-inch thick. Butter both sides, rub both sides with grated Parmesan cheese, then cut in half-inch cubes. Place in a pie tin in a 250-degree oven until browned. These make wonderful croutons for hot, clear venison soup.

Venison Soup Habitant

In northern Quebec they make a venison pea soup that I cannot ignore. It is simplicity itself. In a large kettle soak four cups of split peas in two quarts of salt water. Leave overnight, then drain off the water and add 1 pound of dice venison scraps, ½ pound of salt pork diced in half-inch cubes, two diced carrots, four diced onions, two diced cloves of garlic and four quarts of water. Salt and pepper to taste. Bring to a boil, reduce to a low simmer, and cook for three hours, stirring about every half-hour. Up there they merely add more split peas, more venison, more onion, more carrot, more garlic, more pork and more water each day, and it rests on the back of the stove 24 hours a day. At the first sign of spring you are eating a tiny bit of the same soup that was started the past fall. If you wonder what the cooking odor is when you enter a habitant farmhouse kitchen — that's it. But don't get the idea it isn't delicious — and strengthening.

8
Rabbits and Hares

For every sportsman who hunts grouse, pheasants, quail, waterfowl or big game, there are at least a hundred who hunt rabbits. And of the hundred who hunt rabbits, ninety-nine consider there is but one way to prepare them — *fried!* I bow to no one in my appreciation for properly fried rabbit, but there *are* a few other methods of presenting this meat, and tasty ones.

With the modern interest in diet as a means of reducing weight, it is surprising that several volumes have not appeared devoted solely to the cooking of rabbits, for you could eat rabbit three meals a day for the next six months and you wouldn't gain a pound. According to the experts, this meat has as much food value as so much cotton. However, I might point out at this time that this volume is not intended for those individuals who are worried about gaining the odd ounce or two. There are special volumes for those who feel they must diet. There are a few of the rabbit recipes in this chapter that will provide you with a minimum of this so-called "food value." There are several others that, because of the method of preparation, will give you as much "git-up-and-git" as an equal bulk in beef, pork or lamb. Or almost.

A few years ago a mad French doctor inoculated the rabbits on his estate with a virulent disease that has eliminated something like 90 per cent of the rabbits on the Continent and in England. Although these animals fell into the pest category in some areas, they were a godsend in others, for rabbit was the poor man's beef in many parts of Europe. The French consumed great quantities of this meat, and have felt its loss keenly. For some reason the majority of the hares, fortunately, were immune to the disease, but they have not increased proportionately.

Properly prepared, both rabbit and hare provide excellent dishes. The French, Germans and Scandanavians spent several hundred years experimenting with this meat, and they evolved some exceptional recipes. Jugged hare, for example, is prepared in at least fifty different ways, and all of them that I have tried have been excellent. Both rabbits and hares provide excellent barbecue and casserole dishes, and there are quite a few interesting methods of serving them "fried."

James Burton, who now has a large Eastern automobile agency, began his automotive career in Cheyenne, Wyoming, at a time when sales were few, the pay was low, and rabbits plentiful. "I learned that there were several ways of cooking rabbits," he explains, "but few of them can beat Hasen Pfeffer if it is properly prepared."

HOW TO COOK

At least 24 hours before cooking, prepare the following marinade. In an earthenware casserole place 1 pint of wine vinegar, 2 onions sliced fine, one minced clove of garlic, 4 cloves, 1 bay leaf, 1 shredded carrot, ½ teaspoon of tarragon, ¼ teaspoon of basil, 1 teaspoon of salt. Stir thoroughly and add two rabbits cut in sections. Marinate for 24 hours, turning several times. Marinate in a cool place rather than the refrigerator. Place ⅙ pound of butter in a large skillet and after rubbing dried rabbit sections with salt and pepper, sauté until browned, then add two onions minced fine and brown them lightly. Then add one cup of the strained marinade, place a lid on the skillet, and when it has cooked out, over a medium flame, add another half-cup of marinade. After ten minutes remove rabbit sections to a warming oven and stir in 1 cup of browned breadcrumbs and one cup of sour cream, stirring until gravy thickens. Replace rabbit sections, stir and serve.

Hasen Pfeffer Burton

Requirements
2 rabbits
4 large onions
4 cloves
⅙ pound of butter
6 peppercorns
1 bay leaf
1 carrot
1 pint of wine vinegar
½ teaspoon of tarragon
¼ teaspoon of basil
1 cup of fine, browned
    breadcrumbs
1 cup of sour cream
salt
pepper
1 clove of garlic

Benton Rale of Los Angeles insists that his two favorite methods of preparing rabbit have cost him his supply of this delicacy. Several of his friends, knowing his liking for rabbit, would present him with two or three upon their return from hunting trips. "They didn't like rabbit, but they would spend a few shells gathering a supply for me," he explained. "To repay their gestures, I'd have them for dinner, and eventually they discovered they were eating game they had provided, and found it so good that they decided to keep it for themselves for the future." The following two recipes are Rale specials.

Rabbit à la Rale

Beanhole Rabbit

Requirements

2 rabbits
⅔ cup of olive oil
2 cloves of garlic
2 1-lb. cans of kidney
    beans
2 cups of tomatoes
2 medium onions
½ teaspoon of chervil
2 pinches of thyme
2 dashes of Tabasco sauce
salt
freshly ground
    black pepper

HOW TO COOK

In a large skillet place ⅔ cup of olive oil and one split clove of garlic. When garlic is browned remove and throw away. Add sections of two rabbits and brown well, then place lid on skillet and continue cooking for five minutes. Remove skillet from heat, remove rabbit sections and cut meat from bones in ½-inch cubes. Return skillet to medium flame and add 2 medium onions chopped fine and one minced clove of garlic. Sauté until onions are lightly browned, then add cubed rabbit meat, 2 cups of diced (canned) tomatoes, ½ teaspoon of chervil, 2 pinches of thyme, salt and pepper, 2 dashed of Tabasco sauce and 2 one-pound cans of kidney beans. Place lid on skillet, reduce flame to simmer and cook for two hours.

Rabbit Burgundy

Requirements

2 rabbits or 1 hare
¼ pound of butter
1 pint of Burgundy
4 shallots
1 cup of diced apple
1 bay leaf
1 large onion
4 cloves
6 peppercorns
¼ teaspoon of tarragon
2 pinches of ginger
2 pinches of thyme
1 cup of button
    mushrooms
salt
pepper

HOW TO COOK

Soak the sections of rabbit (or hare) in the following marinade: 1 pint of Burgundy, 1 cup of diced apple, 1 bay leaf, 1 large onion stuck with four cloves, 6 peppercorns, ¼ teaspoon of tarragon, 2 pinches of ginger, 2 pinches of thyme, 1 teaspoon of salt. The meat sections should be soaked (with occasional stirring) for at least eight hours in a cool room. Remove and dry the rabbit sections. In a skillet melt ¼ pound of butter and sauté the rabbit sections until browned, add 4 diced shallots, place lid on skillet and sauté over low flame for five minutes. Place rabbit sections in a casserole, pour butter and shallots over them, then cover with marinade and herbs, add 1 cup of button mushrooms, and placing lid on casserole, put in 350 degree oven for 1½ hours.

This is one of Colonel George L. King's specialties, and it has, according to George, converted many a non-rabbit eater into a steady customer for bunnies.

Rabbit Paprika

HOW TO COOK

Melt ⅙ pound of butter in a large skillet and add one split clove of garlic. When garlic has browned, remove and throw it away. Dust rabbit sections with flour and sauté until browned well, then add 1 cup of chicken stock, 1 cup of rosé wine, 1 pinch of thyme, ¼ teaspoon of basil, 2 minced shallots, salt and pepper, then place lid on skillet and simmer slowly for 1 hour or until rabbit is tender. Remove rabbit to warming oven and add 1 tablespoon of paprika to skillet, stir and scrape skillet well, then stir in one cup of sour cream, stirring it until thick gravy forms. Return rabbit sections to skillet, stir, replace lid and simmer very slowly for two minutes. Remove and serve.

Requirements
2 rabbits or 1 hare
⅙ pound of butter
1 tablespoon of paprika
1 cup of chicken stock
　(or consommé)
1 cup of rosé wine
1 clove of garlic
1 pinch of thyme
¼ teaspoon of basil
2 shallots
1 cup of sour cream
salt
pepper
½ cup of flour

This one comes from the kitchen of Carl Schneider of Madison, Wisconsin, with whom I have argued as to the misnomer involved. Carl uses ale rather than beer in preparing this dish. His only excuse is that "Beery Hare" sounds better than "Aley Hare," and "you can use beer anyway, in a pinch." You may despise beer as a beverage, but you will like Beery Hare.

Beery Hare

HOW TO COOK

In a large casserole place 1 bottle of ale, 1 minced clove of garlic, 1 teaspoon of salt, ¼ teaspoon of pepper, 1 bay leaf, 4 medium-sized onions slice thin, one grated carrot, ¼ teaspoon of allspice, ¼ teaspoon of ground nutmeg. Stir well, and in this marinate one hare cut in serving sections (or two rabbits). Place casserole in the refrigerator for 24 hours, stirring occasionally. In a large skillet melt ½ cup of bacon grease. Place ½ cup of flour, salt and pepper in a brown-paper bag. Shake the hare sections in the bag with flour until well dusted. Sauté in the bacon grease until well browned, then pour marinade (including herbs and vegetables) in skillet and simmer with a lid on the skillet, for 1½ hours. Peel six small potatoes and cut in ¼-inch-thick slices. Cover the hare with the sliced potatoes, replace lid, and simmer for another half hour. Serve with a husky salad of lettuce and tomatoes and plenty of cold beer — or ale.

Requirements
1 large hare or two rabbits
1 bottle of ale (pint)
1 clove of garlic
4 medium-sized onions
1 bay leaf
¼ teaspoon of allspice
　(powdered)
¼ teaspoon of ground
　nutmeg
½ cup of flour
½ cup of bacon grease
6 small potatoes
salt
pepper
1 carrot

Jugged Hare

Requirements

1 large hare or 2 rabbits
12 small white onions
1 large red onion
1 clove of garlic
6 small carrots
½ cup of diced apple
1 bay leaf
¼ teaspoon of basil
2 pinches of thyme
6 cloves
1 pint of dry white wine
1-inch cube of beef suet
2 tablespoons of chopped
    parsley
¼ teaspoon of rosemary
2 pinches of ginger
salt
pepper

This recipe was brought from Belgium by the late J. M. Hardy and prepared by him for the Gourmet and Wine Club on several occasions. Being partial to both rabbit and hare, Hardy explained that he had collected more than twenty recipes for jugged hare, of which this was his favorite.

HOW TO COOK

In a saucepan place 1 pint of dry white wine, 1 large red onion sliced thin, 1 bay leaf, ¼ teaspoon of basil, 6 cloves, 2 pinches of ginger, 1 teaspoon of salt, ¼ teaspoon of freshly ground black pepper. Bring to a boil over a hot fire and allow to boil lightly for one minute. Remove and cool thoroughly. In a tall earthenware casserole (bean pot preferred) place the hare (or rabbits) cut in serving pieces, pour the cooled marinade over it, cover with lid and allow to marinate for 24 hours. After marination pour the contents of the casserole into the kettle. In the bottom of the casserole place a one-inch cube of suet, 12 small white onions, 6 small carrots cut in two-inch lengths, ½ cup of diced apple, 1 minced clove of garlic, 2 pinches of thyme, 2 tablespoons of chopped parsley, ¼ teaspoon of rosemary, then cover with the rabbit sections. Strain the marinade and pour over the rabbit. Put the lid on the casserole and place in a 300-degree oven for 2 hours or until tender. Instead of using large carrots, Hardy would shop the foreign markets until he located 18 tiny 1½-inch carrots, and usually he managed to get fresh basil and rosemary.

Vurn Tracy, who has spent some sixty-eight years in the Maine woods, has never been able to keep a housekeeper for any length of time, so he learned to cook in self-defense. Vurn would much rather eat other people's cooking "if it's fitten to eat," but if it isn't he can turn to and do a fine job on game. It has been rumored, along Tunk River, that he eats very little meat other than game, but the game wardens have never been able to prove it. Vurn has a few herbs, and knows how to use them. Among his seasonings is Jamaica ginger, which is included in this recipe, but I substituted powdered ginger. Safer!

Fried Rabbit Tracy

Requirements

2 rabbits (snowshoes)
¼ pound of salt pork
2 onions
2 tablespoons of flour
3 cloves
1 pinch of powdered ginger
1 cup of milk
salt
pepper

HOW TO COOK

Cut ¼ pound of salt pork (skin removed) into ½-inch cubes, place in a large skillet and render out the fat. When the cubes are brown and crisped, remove to a piece of brown paper to drain. Rub rabbit sections with salt and pepper and sauté in the salt pork fat until browned and tender, dropping three cloves in the pan at the same time the rabbit goes in. Remove the rabbit to a warming oven, remove the cloves, and pour off all the grease except about three tablespoons, add 2 tablespoons of flour slowly and stir over a medium flame until brown, then add two large onions diced fine and one inch of powdered ginger. When onions are browned and tender, stir in one-half cup of water and one cup of milk, stirring until thick gravy is formed, replace rabbit sections and the crisp cubes of salt pork, stir well and serve. Something does *something*, for it is the most delicious "fried" rabbit I have ever tasted. Vurn likes this for breakfast with Aroostook County boiled potatoes, blueberry pie, a few baked beans, and plenty of "boiled" coffee. Unless you have climbed Tunk Mountain the day before and plan climbing it again that day, this proves to be something of a heavy breakfast. Good, though!

Rabbit Stew Hunter Style

Requirements

2 rabbits (or 1 hare)
5 cups of water
2 teaspoons of salt
4 large onions
4 stalks of celery
⅙ pound of butter
2 tablespoons of parsley
6 small apples
6 small potatoes
¼ teaspoon of chervil
1 pinch of thyme
1 cup of cider
1¼ cups of rabbit stock
pepper

This was one of my father's favorite hunting-camp stews. There were always rabbits, even when other game was scarce or difficult to find, and even though rabbit "doesn't stick to your bones," it makes fine eating. Also, this stew could be prepared in stages, if necessary. The initial stewing could be done on the back of the big wood range, which held its heat long enough to finish this process. The second step could be taken an hour or so before dinner.

HOW TO COOK

In a large kettle place 2 rabbits cut in sections, 5 cups of water, 4 stalks of celery, 1 large onion diced fine, ¼ teaspoon of chervil, 2 teaspoons of salt. Bring to a boil, then simmer slowly for 2½ hours. Remove rabbit from stock, then strain stock and save. Cut the meat in thin strips and put to one side. Cut three large onions in thin slices, peel six small apples and cut in ¼-inch slices, peel six small potatoes and cut in ¼-inch slices. Butter an earthenware casserole and put a layer of onions, a layer of rabbit, a layer of apples and a layer of potatoes, dotting each layer with butter and a pinch of pepper. Build up the casserole in these layers, sprinkling a few pinches of chopped parsley over each layer and dotting the final layer with the remainder of the butter and one pinch of thyme. Over this pour 1 cup of cider and 1½ cups of rabbit stock. Place the cover on the casserole and put in a 300-degree oven for one hour.

A friend who made an interesting tour of France after entering the country at a point known to history as Omaha Beach was unable to make up his mind whether he liked the cooking of northern France better than that of the south, but he insists that there is no group of people better versed in the preparation of rabbit and hare than the Normans. "I never realized there were as many means of preparing one kind of meat," he explained, "but if you want to try a really *different* method, cook up some Rabbit Normandy." I can vouch for the truth of this.

HOW TO COOK

Beat up two eggs and ½ cup of milk in a bowl and put in a shallow dish. Place ½ cup of flour in a pie tin, and ½ cup of cornmeal in another pie tin. Dip the sections of rabbit in the milk-egg mixture, then in the flour, then in the milk-egg mixture, then in the cornmeal. Sprinkle the sections with salt and pepper and put them to one side for 10 to 15 minutes. In a large skillet melt ¾ cup of bacon grease and over a low flame brown one shallot sliced in three or four pieces. Remove the shallot and throw it away. Sauté the rabbit in the bacon grease until well browned, reduce the flame, and pour one cup of cider and one cup of Calvados (or applejack) over the rabbit, place a lid on the skillet, and simmer *very* slowly until the liquid has been absorbed or evaporated. Incidentally, if you don't happen to consume it all at one sitting, which is doubtful, it is also delicious cold. After my first trial I made twice as much, just to insure that there would be some to eat cold.

Rabbit Normandy

Requirements
2 rabbits
¾ cup of bacon grease
½ cup of flour
½ cup of cornmeal
½ cup of milk
2 eggs
1 shallot
1 cup of cider
1 cup of Calvados
    (or applejack)
salt
pepper

9
Squirrel

THERE ARE a half-dozen varieties of the animals we call "gray squirrel," and there is no state in which they are not present in greater or lesser numbers. Since the early colonial days they have been high on the game list, and the epicure considers them far superior to rabbit in flavor. Unlike rabbits, they do not adapt well to confinement, and are rarely available in the market.

I have known many hunters who, while seeking other game, will bring down a few squirrels in passing, with the explanation that "Bob likes them, so I always bring him a few when I get a chance." When questioned as to whether they have ever "tried" squirrel they shake their heads. It would be safe to bet that less than half of American shooters ever tasted squirrel, although most of them could have brought home from twenty to a hundred in the course of a season's hunting. They don't know what they are missing.

I have known others who, after trying squirrel for the first time, devoted a good part of the hunting season to the pursuit of this game, and kept a good supply in the deep-freeze.

Many of the early, hand-written recipe books which have been passed down through the generations contain several methods of preparing squirrel, and I was surprised to find that in several I have seen, the use of wine was required in the preparation.

In the future, should a hunting friend offer you a few squirrels, accept them with thanks, but don't invite the donor when you serve the squirrel, for the chances are he will not be so generous in the future.

This is something of a variation of the well-known Brunswick Stew, but, in my opinion, superior to it. During the many years I wrote the Wood, Field and Stream column in *The New York Times* I occasionally printed a recipe for game. Often this brought a sack of mail from sportsmen-chefs who wanted to share one of their favorite methods of preparing that particular bird or animal. Many of these recipes were promising, and I tried them. This one came from T. V. Albury of Columbus, Ohio, and I found it especially awarding.

Squirrel Stew Albury

Requirements
6 squirrels
1 pheasant
3 medium-sized onions
1 cup of flour
1 clove of garlic
¼ pound of butter
2 cups of tomatoes
2 cups of fresh lima beans
2 cups of corn sliced from the cob (or canned corn)
3 cloves
4 sprigs of celery
¼ teaspoon of basil
½ teaspoon of paprika
2 dashes of Tabasco sauce
salt
freshly ground
      black pepper

HOW TO COOK

Cut six squirrels and one pheasant into serving portions, rub with salt and pepper, dust with flour. In a large skillet melt ¼ pound of butter and in it sauté one split clove of garlic until it is browned, then remove garlic and throw away. Sauté squirrel and pheasant until lightly browned. Place in a large kettle and add 2 cups of tomatoes, 3 medium-sized onions chopped fine, 4 sprigs of celery, ¼ teaspoon of basil, 2 dashes of Tabasco sauce, 3 cloves, salt and pepper, and one quart of boiling water. Bring to a boil, reduce heat to a simmer, and place a lid on the kettle. When the squirrel and pheasant are tender remove them from the kettle and cut the meat from the bones, putting the meat to one side. Return the bones to the kettle with the stock and cook until the liquid is reduced to about one pint. Strain through a sieve and return the stock to the kettle, adding the squirrel and pheasant meat, 2 cups of fresh lima beans, 2 cups of corn sliced from the cob, ½ teaspoon of paprika, and simmer slowly for 30 minutes. Serve with white rice, hot cornbread and a tossed green salad.

Note

I have tried stirring in two tablespoons of Espagnol sauce just before removing the kettle from the fire and found it did *something* to the dish.

Squirrel Casserole
Fours

Requirements

4 squirrels
4 medium-sized onions
4 potatoes
4 carrots
4 slices of bacon
4 very thin slices of ham
4 ounces (I added this
    quantity) of applejack
4 pinches of salt (big
    pinches, or 1 teaspoon)
4 ounces of cider
4 pinches of pepper
4 tablespoons of flour

This recipe must have evolved through the meditations of a numerologist, but it was passed on to me by an Adirondack guide who could barely count and whose reading was limited to the almanack and the mail-order catalogue. It is reliably reported that he had never been able to read the fine print in the game-law booklet. He guided anglers in the spring and summer, hunters in the fall, and cut pulpwood in the winter. The recipe, he explained, was one that was "handed down." I now carry on the tradition by handing it down, for it is worth it.

HOW TO COOK

Cut four large squirrels into serving portions, rub them with salt and pepper. In the bottom of an earthenware casserole (one with a tight-fitting lid) arrange 4 very thin slices of ham, then arrange a layer of squirrel, then a layer of thinly sliced onion, a layer of thinly sliced carrot and a layer of thinly sliced potato, and build up the casserole in similar layers, sprinkling each with salt and pepper to taste. Over this arrange four strips of bacon. Add four ounces of cider and four ounces of applejack, place the lid on the casserole and seal the lid with a paste made of flour and water. (My mentor, after putting the casserole in the oven, weighted it with a tremendous flatiron, to insure the seal.) Place the casserole in a 250-degree oven for three hours. My mentor, after removing the lid and plunking the casserole in the middle of the table, announced: "This'll stick to your ribs, an' it's damn good too." He was right on both counts.

Bob Lane, who invested in several tracts of "submarginal" farms lands on the Mississippi, found he had acquired an abundance of ducks, turkeys, squirrels and rabbits along with a glassless but otherwise sound farmhouse. "A little over a hundred years ago, I understand," he would explain, "the westward-ho outfits crossed the river not far from here. When they reached the Arkansas side there were two signs. One read: 'Texas that way.' The other read: 'California that way.' Those who could read took one of these two trails, the others stopped in Arkansas." With this kind of hunting, I don't blame them! Bob was not only a good hand with a squirrel rifle and a shotgun, but he had a real *touch* with a skillet.

In addition to his other culinary accomplishments he made the best spoon bread anyone ever tasted. His Fried Squirrel Arkansas was so good that his guests always pressured him into repeat performances.

HOW TO COOK

In a large saucepan place 1 cup of chicken stock, 1 cup of dry white wine, 1 medium-sized onion minced fine, 2 pinches of rosemary, 1 tablespoon of chopped parsley, salt and pepper to taste, and four squirrels cut in serving portions. Bring to a boil, reduce heat to a simmer and cook for ten minutes. Remove squirrel sections and put to one side, allowing the stock to continue simmering. Beat up 2 eggs and place in a shallow pan, and place one cup of yellow cornmeal in a similar pan. Roll the squirrel sections in egg, then in cornmeal. Put to one side for ten minutes, then roll in egg and cornmeal for a second time. In a large skillet melt ¼ pound of butter and in it brown one split clove of garlic, then remove garlic and throw it away. Brown the squirrel sections in butter until tender, then remove to a warming oven. Remove the stock from the fire, strain it, and add ⅔ of a cup to the skillet, stirring and scraping over a low flame until the gravy thickens. Serve the gravy separately, over rice or grits.

Fried Squirrel Arkansas

Requirements
4 squirrels
2 eggs
1 cup of cornmeal
1 cup of chicken stock
1 cup of dry white wine
1 clove of garlic
1 medium-sized onion
2 pinches of rosemary
¼ pound of butter
1 tablespoon of chopped
    parsley
salt
freshly ground black
    pepper

Wild Acres Squirrel

Requirements
4 "young" squirrels
   (you hope)
1 pint of milk
2 eggs
½ cup of flour
1 kettle with 2 inches of
   vegetable oil inside

This recipe came to me via Lurton "Count" Blassingame, who likes to hunt, fish, eat, and labor with his stable of outdoor writers to the point where they also are assured of eating. There must be something about Arkansas that stimulates squirrel-eating, for this one also comes from that state, and the kitchen of W. H. Claypool of Wild Acres Farm.

HOW TO COOK

Cut four squirrels in serving portions and soak them in 1 pint of milk for a half hour. Meanwhile prepare a batter by beating 2 eggs, then stirring in ½ cup of flour. Add enough milk to create a fairly thick batter. Dip the squirrels in the batter until thoroughly coated and drop them in the kettle of hot oil. (The oil temperature should be about 350 degrees, which means it would take 60 seconds to brown a one-inch cube of bread). When the squirrel sections are well browned, remove and drain on brown paper or paper towel in warming oven.

Squirrel Marsala

Requirements
4 squirrels
1 cup of chicken stock
2 small onions
1 tablespoon of parsley
½ cup of white wine
1 lemon
¼ pound of butter
1 carrot
¼ teaspoon of chervil
1 pinch of marjoram
¼ cup of Marsala
1 cup of sour cream
salt
freshly ground
   black pepper

This is a somewhat exotic recipe to come from Maine, but it arrived via Elmore Wallace, a former Sea and Shore Fisheries Warden who "had it from a friend who knew a man who cooked for an ex-prince." The whole situation is complicated, but Elmore is not, and the recipe is truly different.

HOW TO COOK

In a saucepan place 1 cup of chicken stock, ½ cup of dry white wine, 1 tablespoon of parsley, 1 grated carrot, 2 minced onions, ¼ teaspoon of chervil, 1 pinch of marjoram and bring to a boil. Reduce heat to simmer, place lid on saucepan and simmer for 30 minutes. Force through a sieve and put stock to one side. In a large skillet melt ¼ pound of butter and in it sauté four squirrels that have been cut in serving sections and rubbed with salt and pepper. Sauté over medium flame until well browned, reduce to low heat and add the stock, scraping and stirring. Place a cover on the skillet and simmer for 10 minutes, stirring occasionally. Stir in the juice of one lemon, ¼ cup of Marsala, and simmer for 5 minutes without cover. Stir in one cup of sour cream, salt and pepper to taste, then place in chafing dish over low alcohol flame.

This was a recipe of my grandmother's that was always a favorite. When I managed to load the back of my shooting coat with squirrels, my first hopeful stop, as a youngster, was at Grandma's, where I would try to trade off the day's bag for a promise of Squirrel Pie. It is a simple, but to my mind, magnificent dish.

HOW TO COOK

In a saucepan place 1 cup of chicken stock, ½ cup of cider, ¼ teaspoon of rosemary, 1 pinch of ginger, 1 tablespoon of chopped parsley, 2 small apples diced, 2 large onions diced, 3 carrots cut in ¼-inch-thick rounds, bring to a boil, then reduce flame to a simmer, place lid on saucepan, and simmer for 20 minutes. In a large skillet place ¼ pound of salt pork cut in ½-inch cubes. Render salt pork over a medium flame until cubes are crisp, remove cubes and drain on brown paper. Cut four squirrels into serving portions, rub with pepper, dust with flour, and brown in the salt pork fat. Prepare enough pie crust to line a large (12- by 3-inch) earthenware casserole and to cover the top of the casserole. Grease the casserole with some of the salt pork fat and line it with pie crust. Arrange the browned squirrel pieces on the bottom crust and sprinkle the browned salt pork cubes over them. Meanwhile, when the stock-onions-apples-carrots have simmered 20 minutes, add four potatoes, each potato divided in six parts, and simmer for an additional ten minutes without the cover on the saucepan. Spoon the contents of the saucepan over the squirrel, place the top crust on the casserole, and put in an oven preheated to 350 degrees. Bake until crust is browned, and serve.

Squirrel Pie

Requirements

4 squirrels
3 carrots
2 large onions
   (preferably red)
2 apples (small)
4 medium-sized potatoes
¼ pound of salt pork
1 tablespoon of chopped
   parsley
1 pinch of ginger
¼ teaspoon of rosemary
1 cup of chicken stock
½ cup of cider
salt
pepper
pie crust

10
Sauces

THERE ARE a number of sauces that should be in every kitchen where good cooking is practiced. Some should be on the shelves in the cupboard, others in the refrigerator. Many home-prepared sauces call for the expenditure of a certain amount of time and effort, but they can be placed in jars, capped, and kept in the refrigerator for weeks — if they last that long.

Many of the recipes included in this book call for certain of these prepared sauces, but they apply only to the cooking of game. For one game dinner, the average household serves twenty-five (or more) in which beef, pork, veal or poultry play the major role. Many of the recipes included herein can be employed for the cooking of these very civilized and domestic meats. Therefore, the various sauces suggested need not be held solely for the occasions when game is on the menu. For example, there are four or five of the major sauces that literally have a thousand uses (or opportunities for use). These include Sauce Espagnol, Béchamel sauce, Bordelaise sauce, Barbecue sauce and Sauce Bernaise.

Many of these sauces can be used on broiled and roast meats, fish, and in the preparation of gravies, to which they give added favor, flavor and zest. It has been definitely established that certain sauces blend more adequately with certain meats and fish, and any good "general" cook book will list their proper usage.

There are some slight variations by various chefs in the actual ingredients and the quantity of ingredients of some of these sauces. I have experimented with some of these variations, and the recipes selected are those I found most acceptable although not necessarily less complicated. I can assure you the time and effort expended in the preparation of these sauces is not wasted.

HOW TO COOK

In a saucepan melt three tablespoons of butter, then blend in 2½ tablespoons of flour, one medium-sized onion minced fine, 1 bay leaf, 1½ teaspoons of salt. Stir constantly over a low flame for eight to ten minutes, then remove the bay leaf. Slowly stir in two cups of milk that has been pre-heated until steam rises from it. Continue to stir sauce for 15 minutes over a low flame. Strain and place in glass jar in refrigerator when cool.

Béchamel Sauce

Requirements

3 tablespoons of butter
2½ tablespoons of flour
6 peppercorns
1½ teaspoons of salt
1 bay leaf
1 medium-sized onion or 3
    shallots
2 cups of milk

HOW TO COOK

In a saucepan melt 3 tablespoons of butter over a medium flame, stir in three tablespoons of flour, then gradually stir in 3 cloves of garlic minced fine, 3 tablespoons of minced onion, 6 stalks of celery diced fine, 2 dashes of Tabasco sauce, 1 bay leaf, 1 teaspoon of salt, 2 cups of beef stock and 1 tablespoon of paprika. Simmer, stirring constantly, for 15 to 20 minutes, then remove from fire, stir in 3 tablespoons of dry sherry and strain. Place in glass jar in refrigerator when cool.

Bordelaise Sauce

Requirements

3 tablespoons of butter
3 tablespoons of flour
3 cloves of garlic
3 tablespoons minced
    onions
6 stalks of celery
2 dashes Tabasco sauce
1 bay leaf
1 tablespoon of paprika
1 teaspoon of salt
3 tablespoons of dry sherry
2 cups of beef stock

Sauce Espagnol

(Complicated, time-consuming, but *important*)

HOW TO COOK

Melt ¼ pound of butter in a large kettle over a medium flame; when butter simmers add 1 cup of diced carrots, 1 cup of finely chopped onions, 3 minced cloves of garlic, 3 tablespoons of chopped parsley, 1 teaspoon of basil, 1 teaspoon of marjoram, 1 cup of chopped celery, 2 bay leaves, 5 crushed peppercorns. Sauté these vegetables and herbs, stirring constantly, until light brown, then remove from fire and put to one side, draining off the butter and saving it in a cup. Place 1 pound of beef bones, 1 pound of veal bones, 1 beef or veal marrowbone and one ham bone in a roasting pan and put into a 450-degree oven until bones have become well browned. Place bones with their drippings in the kettle with the sautéed vegetables and herbs, then add 2 cups of canned tomatoes, 1 cup of Madeira, 12 cups of beef bouillon, 5 cups of water, ½ teaspoon of Tabasco sauce, ½ pound of veal, ½ pound of beef, 1 tablespoon of salt and 3 cloves. Place lid on kettle and simmer contents over a medium flame for 3½ hours, skimming fat from surface of kettle every half hour. Remove kettle from fire and allow to cool to a degree where it is possible to skim all of the fat from the surface, then strain through fine mesh sieve or coarse cheesecloth. In a large saucepan place ¾ of a cup of butter (using some of original butter) and stir in one cup of flour, stirring constantly until flour is browned, then slowly stir in the strained stock. Reduce flame to simmer and stir until stock thickens. Remove from stove and store in glass jars in refrigerator. This supply should last the average household at least two months. (Quart mason jars make excellent containers.)

Requirements

1 pound of beef bones
1 pound of veal bones
1 beef or veal marrowbone
1 ham bone with shreds of
    meat (no fat)
½ pound of veal
½ pound of beef
1 cup of diced carrots
1 cup of chopped onions
3 cloves of garlic
3 tablespoons of chopped
    parsley
1 teaspoon of basil
1 teaspoon of marjoram
1 cup of chopped celery
    (including leaves)
2 bay leaves
5 peppercorns (crushed)
2 cups of canned tomatoes
1 cup of Madeira
12 cups of beef bouillon
5 cups of water
½ teaspoon of Tabasco
    sauce
1 cup of flour
1 tablespoon of salt
¼ pound of butter
3 cloves

Hollandaise Sauce

HOW TO COOK

In the top of a double boiler (preferably one with rounded bottom) place four beaten egg yolks to which has been added 3 tablespoons of water, ½ teaspoon of salt and one pinch of black pepper. In a small saucepan melt ⅙ pound of butter and have ready a glass with 2 tablespoons of lemon juice. Place top of double boiler over the base which is over a moderate flame and begin stirring briskly with a wire whisk. As you stir with one hand pour a light but steady flow of melted butter into the beaten eggs, stirring *constantly*. After butter has been added slowly stir in the two tablespoons of lemon juice, and continue stirring until sauce thickens. When it has reached the consistency of sour cream remove from the base of the double boiler and continue to stir for about one minute. This can be put to one side and warmed up when needed. Many prepare a double portion and keep it in the refrigerator, where it should remain for not more than one week.

Requirements
⅙ pound of butter
4 egg yolks
½ teaspoon of salt
1 pinch of freshly
    ground black pepper
3 tablespoons of water
2 tablespoons of
    lemon juice

Sauce Bearnaise

HOW TO COOK

In a saucepan place all of the ingredients and simmer gently until approximately three tablespoons of fluid remain in the pan. Allow it to cool, then prepare Hollandaise sauce as previously explained, beating the fluid and herbs into the eggs as a substitute for the 3 tablespoons of water, and eliminating the two tablespoons of lemon juice.

Note:

In preparing Hollandaise I prefer to use a three-quart stainless-steel mixing bowl, almost a perfect half-sphere, with only a two-inch flattened area at the base. Such a bowl comes in very handy for making many sauces, as it permits the full use of a whisk. This can be placed over a pan of steaming water in lieu of a double boiler. I have these bowls in two-, three- and four-quart sizes and have found them a worthwhile investment.

Requirements
2 shallots (or tiny white
    onions) minced fine
3 tablespoons of dry
    white wine
½ teaspoon of tarragon
½ teaspoon of chervil
¼ teaspoon of freshly
    ground black pepper
1 tablespoon of vinegar
1 dash of Tabasco sauce
1 teaspoon of minced
    parsley
3 tablespoons of water

Cumberland Sauce

Requirements
½ cup of currant jelly
2 tablespoons of dry
    mustard
1 tablespoon of grated
    orange peel
2 ounces of Madeira
2 tablespoons of lemon
juice
2 tablespoons of sugar
½ teaspoon of powdered
    ginger
2 egg yolks
1 pinch of cayenne pepper
½ teaspoon of salt

HOW TO COOK

Moisten 2 tablespoons of dry mustard with water until it is a smooth paste. In the top of a double boiler melt ½ cup of currant jelly, remove from flame and allow it to cool for about five minutes, then stir in the yolks of two eggs, the mustard paste, 1 tablespoon of grated orange peel, 2 ounces of Madeira, 2 tablespoons of lemon juice, two tablespoons of sugar, 1 pinch of cayenne pepper and ½ teaspoon of salt. Blend thoroughly with a whisk, then place over flame and bring to a boil, reduce the flame and simmer for about ten minutes, stirring constantly with the wisk. Remove from fire and serve either hot or cold.

Velouté Sauce

Requirements
1 medium-sized onion
1 teaspoon of salt
2½ tablespoons of flour
3 tablespoons of butter
1 bay leaf
6 peppercorns

This is a basic sauce for fish, meat or vegetables when served "creamed." To it can be added the stock of essence in which the meat or vegetables have been prepared. If to be used as a sauce for fish, court bouillon is added. Professional chefs always have a supply of this on hand.

HOW TO COOK

Melt 3 tablespoons of butter in a saucepan and stir in 2½ tablespoons of flour, one medium-sized minced onion, 1 bay leaf and 6 peppercorns. Stir constantly over a very low flame for about ten minutes. Then stir in two tablespoons of the stock to be used and simmer over a low flame for 15 minutes, then remove and strain.

While this is a favored sauce for fish, many chefs also serve it over fowl.

HOW TO COOK

Sauté 1 medium-sized onion, minced fine, in 3 tablespoons of butter in a small saucepan, then add 1 cup of dry white wine, ½ cup of diced tomatoes, ½ teaspoon of prepared mustard, ½ teaspoon of sugar, 1 tablespoon of lemon juice and ½ teaspoon of salt. Simmer slowly for at least twenty minutes.

Note:

It is common practice to add one-half cup of Sauce Espagnol to the above. For example, an excellent quick snack can be prepared by placing a half-inch-thick slice of cold roast venison on a piece of toast, covering it with four or five tablespoons of this sauce and sliding it under the broiler for three or four minutes.

White Wine Sauce

Requirements

1 medium-sized onion, minced fine
½ cup of diced tomatoes
1 cup of dry white wine
3 tablespoons of butter
½ teaspoon of prepared mustard
½ teaspoon of sugar
1 tablespoon of lemon juice
½ teaspoon of salt

This is another sauce of many uses, and a number of amateur chefs find it excellent for basting grilled game, both venison and fowl, and it is especially tasty for basting grilled rabbit or hare.

HOW TO COOK

Place all of the ingredients in a saucepan and simmer over a lower flame for 30 minutes with a lid on the pan. Force through a fine sieve and store in glass jar in refrigerator. It will keep indefinitely.

Quick Barbecue Sauce

Requirements

4 large onions, minced fine
3 cloves of garlic, minced fine
½ cup of olive oil
½ cup of tomato catsup
1 large bay leaf
½ teaspoon of marjoram
1 teaspoon of celery salt
½ teaspoon of oregano
¼ teaspoon of Tabasco sauce
¼ teaspoon of powdered allspice
⅔ cup of wine vinegar
1 cup of tomato juice
1 teasoon of salt

Sour Cream Sauce

Requirements
1 cup of sour cream
2 tablespoons of lemon
juice
2 egg yolks
½ teaspoon of salt
1 teaspoon of minced
parsley
1 teaspoon of paprika

HOW TO COOK
Blend all of the ingredients, place in the top of a double boiler over low heat and stir constantly (do not beat) until it thickens.

Burgundy Sauce

Requirements
⅙ pound of butter
2 shallots, minced fine
4 crushed peppercorns
1 bay leaf
1 cup of Burgundy
¼ teaspoon of salt
1 tablespoon of
Worcestershire sauce
8 capers

HOW TO COOK
In a saucepan melt ⅙ pound of butter and add 2 shallots minced fine, 4 crushed peppercorns, 1 crushed bay leaf, and sauté over low flame until lightly browned, then add 1 cup of Burgundy, ¼ teaspoon of salt, 1 tablespoon of Worcestershire sauce and 8 capers. Simmer for 15 minutes then strain. Add one cup of Espagnole sauce, simmer for five minutes.

Mornay Sauce

Requirements
2 egg yolks
2 tablespoons of dry sherry
3 tablespoons of grated
sharp cheese
2 tablespoons of grated
Parmesan cheese
1 tablespoon of butter
¼ teaspoon of salt
1 cup of Béchamel sauce

HOW TO COOK
In a saucepan blend 1 cup of Béchamel sauce with two beaten egg yolks, 2 tablespoons of dry sherry, 3 tablespoons of grated sharp cheese, 2 tablespoons of grated Parmesan cheese, 1 tablespoon of butter and ¼ teaspoon of salt. Simmer lightly over a low flame, stirring constantly, until ingredients are smoothly blended (about five minutes).

Curry Sauce

HOW TO COOK

In a saucepan melt ¼ pound of butter and stir in two large onions, minced fine. Sauté over a low flame until onions are lightly browned, then stir in 4 tablespoons of flour and sauté for about three minutes. To this add 2 cups of chicken stock, stirring briskly, one cup of Madeira, 3 tablespoons of lemon juice, 2 tablespoons of curry powder, 1 large bay leaf, ½ teaspoon of salt, 6 peppercorns, ¼ teaspoon of grated nutmeg, and simmer over a low flame for ten minutes, or until it begins to thicken. Strain and serve hot or cold.

Requirements

¼ pound of butter
2 large onions
6 peppercorns
¼ tablespoons grated nutmeg
1 large bay leaf
4 tablespoons of flour
3 tablespoons of lemon juice
½ teaspoon of salt
2 cups of chicken stock
1 cup of Madeira
2 tablespoons of curry powder

Mushroom Sauce

HOW TO COOK

In a saucepan melt 3 tablespoons of butter, add 1½ cups of diced mushrooms and sauté until lightly browned, over a low flame. Add ¼ cup of tomato juice, 4 tablespoons of dry sherry, ½ teaspoon of salt, and simmer slowly, stirring constantly, for about two minutes. Then stir in one cup of Espagnol sauce and simmer over a low flame for 10 minutes. Remove from fire, stir in one tablespoon of chopped parsley and serve.

Requirements

1½ cups of diced mushrooms
3 tablespoons of butter
1 tablespoon of chopped parsley
½ teaspoon of salt
¼ cup of tomato juice
4 tablespoons of dry sherry
1 cup of Espagnol sauce

Stock

There are always many uses for stock in every kitchen, and there are no kitchens where material for stock is not available. The stock pot itself, except in restaurant kitchens, has gone out with the coal range, but in every kitchen there are leftover vegetables, meats, bones and such items as celery and beet tops. Collect these in one of the plastic refrigerator boxes for two days and you have enough for about a quart of good stock. The normal rule-of-thumb is twice the amount of water for the amount of raw material, then reduce by two thirds. When you buy your meat, make a habit of asking the butcher for a few bones. He will be glad to provide them, and they will, with what accumulates in your refrigerator, form a basis for an excellent stock.

Make it a habit of going through the refrigerator on a certain day each week. Assemble the bits and pieces of vegetables: a couple of carrots, a half-head of lettuce, a few stalks of celery, and similar items. Add the bones provided by the butcher, a couple of onions, a half-teaspoon of salt, and put them with about three quarts of water in a large kettle. Simmer it until the liquid is reduced by two thirds, strain it, and put it aside to cool. Skim the fat from the top, and store in a refrigerator jar with cap. If you wish, you can very easily clarify it. Wash an egg, put the yolk in the refrigerator, then add the white and the broken shells to the strained, skimmed stock. Bring it slowly to a boil in a saucepan, let it boil for two minutes, then strain it through a piece of muslin or cheesecloth. You will have a fine, clear stock. There are many ways in which your routine dishes can be improved through use of this stock. In game cookery, it is most important.

11
"Along Withs"

THERE ARE certain dishes that seem to be a natural accompaniment to game. None of them is difficult to prepare, but a few of the simplest ones seem to cause trouble in some kitchens. In the South, because of its wide use, rice is inevitably properly cooked. For some reason, the rice turned out by many of the Northern cooks is soggy, mushy and inclined to adhere to the roof of the mouth. Rice cookery should follow a firm and definite routine if the result is to be a light, palatable dish. In view of this I will put down the foolproof methods of cooking rice, both white and wild.

White Rice

Place one cup of white rice in a large saucepan, and let water run into it and overflow. Scrub the rice two or three minutes under this cold, flowing water. Place it in a sieve and wash it under the tap. Then shake as much water from it as possible and put it aside to drain for about 10 minutes. Bring 1½ cups of salted water to a boil, stir in the rice and when the water again comes to a boil, reduce the flame to a *very low* simmer, place a lid on the saucepan and in fifteen minutes you have light, fluffy rice, each grain separate.

Saffron Rice

Wash and dry one cup of rice as above. In a small saucepan heat up 1½ cups of chicken stock or consommé. Place 6 of the hairlike tendrils of saffron in cup (or powdered saffron the size of a match head) and add one tablespoon of the hot stock. Stir for two or three minutes, then allow the saffron to soak in the stock for ten minutes. Retrieve the tendrils of saffron, pour some of the stock from the saucepan into the cup to thin the liquid, then add the contents of the cup to the saucepan and stir well. In another saucepan melt 2 tablespoons of butter, then add the washed and dried rice, stirring constantly until the rice is a light brown, pour in the boiling saffron stock and stir thoroughly. Reduce the heat to a *low* simmer, place a lid on the pan, and cook for 15 minutes.

Wild Rice

Wash one cup of wild rice in the same manner as given for white rice. Place two cups of salted water in a saucepan and when it boils stir in the rice. Simmer for five minutes, pour off into a sieve, and run cold water over the partially cooked rice for two or three minutes, shake to remove excess water and dry for ten minutes. Bring 1½ cups of chicken stock or consommé to a boil, stir in the rice and when stock again boils, reduce the heat to a *low* simmer, place a lid on the saucepan and simmer for 15 minutes.

Herb Rolls or Bread

In a small mixing bowl blend 1 teaspoon of rosemary, 1 teaspoon of marjoram, ½ teaspoon of basil, ¼ teaspoon of tarragon, 2 pinches of thyme (powder all these herbs in a mortar and pestle if you have one), add ¼ pound of soft butter, and stir until herbs and butter are blended. Make six deep cuts in a large hard roll, bringing the knife down to the bottom crust. Spread the herb butter between these cuts (this does six rolls). Wrap the rolls in aluminum foil and place in a 350-degree oven for 10 minutes. French bread can be prepared in the same manner, cutting across the loaf to about ¼ inch from the bottom crust. Wrap in aluminum foil or place in a heavy brown paper bag if no foil is available.

Garlic Rolls or Bread

Melt ¼ pound of butter in a small saucepan over a *very low* flame, and add two large cloves of garlic split into a half-dozen slices. Simmer the garlic in the butter for five minutes, stirring constantly, and taking care not to brown the butter. Remove the garlic and spread the rolls or French bread with the garlic-flavored butter, using a pastry brush. Cut rolls or French bread in same manner as given in previous recipe.

Chutney Rolls or Bread

Chop *very fine* four tablespoons of Major Grey's Chutney. Place ¼ pound of soft butter in a small mixing bowl and blend in the chopped chutney, then slowly sprinkle and stir in ½ teaspoon of curry powder. Spread on rolls or French bread in same manner as given in previous recipe.

12

The Importance
of Herbs

THE GENERAL use of herbs in cookery has shown a definite upswing
during the past ten years, and small herb gardens have sprung up, not only
in urban flower gardens but in city window boxes. In most of the larger cities
the major herbs used in cookery can be obtained in the "green" form,
although the sources often are difficult to find. Throughout most of the
country, however, the amateur as well as the professional must accept the
dried form.

The importance of herbs in game cookery could not possibly be over-
emphasized. Many of them are *vital* to the proper preparation of the various
dishes. Herbs *compliment* and *enhance* the flavor of the meats, bringing out the
full savory qualities that otherwise would be lost. It cannot be denied that
the *over*-use of herbs can often be more harmful than not using them at all.
There are a number of pungent herbs that must be handled with restraint,

for while a *hint* of their flavor is a real benison, a hefty pinch can be a disaster. The two herbs most commonly *mis*used are sage and saffron. Both are extremely pungent and must be used with precision. Everyone has heard the expression "There is no such thing as a *little* garlic." Despite this statement, many who claim to possess highly sensitive noses and taste buds are unable to detect garlic when it is properly used.

American cooks have never been as educated in the use of herbs as those of other countries. This may be attributed to the fact that our early settlers were primarily English, and the English never advanced as far in herb cookery as did their Latin neighbors, or even their Scandinavian relatives. It is charged that the English never advanced as far in cookery, period, and anyone who has spent any length of time in England will agree that their food can be described, for the most part as *plain*. Roast beef, mutton and pork, fried, boiled or roasted, and with speed rather than care in preparation. During their recent period of austerity, however, when meat was rigidly rationed, they did advance considerably in the use of herbs. Since so little was available, they apparently decided to get the most out of that little.

The increased interest in good food, and in the use of herbs in cookery, in American homes can be ascribed, I believe, to education. As Americans had more leisure to spend in travel they encountered new methods of preparing food. Several million Americans enjoyed all-expense tours to foreign parts during World War II, and having tasted the food of other countries and found it good, they decided it was time they educated the home folks. I know of countless instances where this occurred. More men learn to cook during a war than at any other time. At any rate, there is an herb revival in the United States, so let's relax and enjoy it.

Among the herbs which should be on the shelf in every kitchen are the following. But before listing them, with their application, I want to make one more point. Freshly ground pepper gives an added zest to any food. Pepper pots can be had at prices ranging from 25¢ to $125. The 25¢ pepper mill will do the job adequately, even though it is less ornate. Peppercorns are available at any grocery today, and any good hardware store carries pepper mills.

There are a number of reliable firms now engaged in packaging herbs, some in tins, some in glass. I prefer the glass container with a metal screw lid. There are three sources I prefer — House of Herbs, Bellows and Co., and Spice Islands. These producers use care in the curing and packaging of their products, which is extremely important.

BASIL

This is a rather pungent herb, but it has the faculty of blending well with meats, fish and vegetables, and it is not necessary to be as guarded in its use as is the case with some other herbs. If it can be obtained fresh, it is worth the added effort. With the exception of dill, it is probably used more with vegetables than any other herb. It is important in many sauces.

BAY

The bay leaf has been used in cookery since time immemorial and needs no explanation here. It is, however, more pungent than it appears to be, and few dishes call for the use of more than one small bay leaf.

CHERVIL

This is one of the more subtle herbs, and except when used in the fresh form usually is employed in combination with one or more other herbs. It has a delicate flavor and it is not necessary to use great care in adding it to the pot. Even as much as a quarter teaspoon over the requirement will not seriously affect the dish.

CHIVE

This is a most important herb, but can be used only in the green form. Fortunately, it can be grown in a can or flower pot on the window sill in any climate, and grows in lush profusion. There is hardly a dish that does not benefit from a sprinkling of chopped chives at the time of serving. Although an onion relative, it is less harsh than onion, and blends perfectly with many other herbs. *Every* house should have a pot of chives.

DILL

This is one of the most widely used herbs in cookery, but it is difficult to obtain fresh except in the larger markets, and many are forced to use it in the form of powdered dill seed. It can be readily grown in any climate, however, and can be grown indoors, although it is a rather large plant. It is undoubtedly the number one herb in all Scandinavian countries. It is a real asset to any stew, is fine on fish, important in sauces and salads, and adds a piquant touch to most vegetables. It should be present in the powdered seed form on your herb shelf.

MARJORAM

Here is another of the really important herbs that has an almost universal use in the kitchen. It is a mild herb, but one which blends well with others. It is widely used on both meats and vegetables, but not too often with fish. It retains its fragrance after being properly dried. Can be used quite liberally.

OREGANO

This is an herb that has been basic in Latin kitchens for centuries, and without it many of the Italian, Spanish and South American dishes would lack much of their flavor. It is a stout herb, and while strong, tends to blend well. It should be used with reasonable care, although it is not in the sage and saffron category. It is used generally on meat and fish, is important to many sauces and dressings, and especially vital in many stews. It is not widely used with vegetables.

PARSLEY

This herb needs no introduction to the American cook, but in many instances it could be more widely used than it now is. It is not as pungent as many others, and for this reason blends with almost any dish, often sacrificing its own flavor to bring out the flavor of other herbs and vegetables. It would be difficult to name many dishes which would not be improved by the judicious use of parsley. Use more of it in your kitchen, for it is available everywhere in the fresh state.

ROSEMARY

This is one of the truly ancient cookery herbs, and has a wide use in the preparation of most meats, although not greatly favored for use with fish or vegetables. While rather pungent, it has a "sweet" perfume and is without harshness. It should, however, be used with reasonable restraint. It is especially good with venison prepared in almost any manner. It seems to lose little fragrance through drying.

SAGE

This is a fine herb, but must be used with *real* restraint. A mere pinch is normally sufficient for a dish that might employ a teaspoon of another herb (except saffron). It is not a new herb to the American cook, but too often it is over-used. I have eaten poultry stuffing that literally *reeked* of this herb, to the extent that other flavors and odors were completely submerged. A "hint" of sage improves many dishes, but make certain that you do not go overboard on the "pinch." Many otherwise good sausages are spoiled by too much sage, and it has only one real friend — the manufacturers of indigestion remedies.

SAVORY

Savory is a "blending" herb, and although it has a pleasant flavor it is not too widely used. It has a tendency to bring out the flavor of other herbs, and is excellent in many sauces and stews.

SAFFRON

This herb has increased in popularity, possibly as a result of increased travel, for it used in many dishes in Latin countries and in the East, both Near and Far. It must be treated with *great* care. If it were not for the real value of this herb in many dishes I would suggest it be eliminated. This, however, would be a definite loss, as the herb has a real part to play in cookery. It comes in two forms: in tiny, hairlike, reddish tendrils, or in a powder. Although the powder is much easier to use, it is far more difficult to measure, so I prefer the tendrils. For a stew sufficient for four persons, for example, I work out five of the hairlike tendrils and soak them in a tablespoon of hot water. In a few minutes the water takes on a yellowish color. Then I *remove* the tendrils of saffron. For a similar dish I use a pinch of powdered saffron the size of the head of a wooden match. This also should be soaked in hot water to insure distribution. Do not forego the use of this herb because of its difficulty in use. It *should* be on your herb shelf.

THYME

This is another of the ancient herbs, but one that is widely used throughout the world. As with many others, it is superior in the fresh state, but undoubtedly 99 per cent of its users have to use it dried. It is one of the great "blending" herbs, and undoubtedly has done more to offset the overpowering odor of sage than any other agent. It is widely used in America, and many thoughtful cooks have substituted it (entirely) for sage in making their poultry dressing. It has a rather pronounced yet subtle flavor and does much to enhance the natural flavors of many meats. It is also quite widely used in fish as well as meat sauces. When used with other herbs it is often extremely difficult, even for an expert, to detect its presence.

Seasonings

GARLIC

Many cooks amateur and professional, would not know what to do without garlic. It is, unquestionably, the number one seasoning agent, and is used, in moderation, in the majority of meat dishes, most sauces, and also, in great moderation, in the preparation of fish. This is one item that is an absolute *must* in all kitchens where an interest is taken in the proper preparation of food. An indispensable item, among utensils, in my opinion, is the garlic "mincer." This resembles a miniature potato ricer, and forces the soft essence of the garlic through the base. It permits the chef to *blend* the garlic perfectly in dishes where the garlic is to remain and not be withdrawn later. Always have *fresh* garlic cloves in your kitchen.

PEPPERCORNS

These are coming into wider use in the American kitchen, although they have been present in European kitchens for ages. They are of real culinary value and importance in most stews and sauces, for during the cooking process they impart to the essences the flavor rather than the physical presence of pepper.

CAPERS

There are a number of game dishes in which capers play a necessary role. They are *not* merely a form of decoration, but impart a distinctive pungent flavor, although this flavor blends well when other herbs are used.

GINGER

Although it is not widely used, even in many of the more elaborate European dishes, ginger in powdered form is called for in a number of recipes, and it undoubtedly adds a tang to many dishes. It is a "blender," although the essence it imparts would be missed. It should be on the seasoning shelf in every kitchen.

CURRY

Curry powder is a powerful seasoning, being a blend of many pungent herbs and spices, and although primarily used in the preparation of curried dishes, a pinch of the powder improves many recipes. It should be used with reasonable caution, but has a definite place on the seasoning shelf.

PAPRIKA

Although much milder than the other peppers, paprika has a definite use beyond its value as a coloring agent. It *has* a flavor, as you would soon realize if you tasted a dish that called for its use and found it had been left out. Hungarian paprika is superior to the Spanish variety, both in flavor and color.

SHALLOTS

This soft-voiced member of the onion family has tremendous importance in the *haute cuisine*. While more pungent than onion it is less penetrating than garlic, and is rapidly gaining in popularity in America, especially among those interested in good cooking. Like chives, shallots can be grown at home, and the average cook who has tried them in a few dishes will go to real lengths in order to locate a supply. They will keep well if placed in a glass jar, and are unquestionably a *must* for the dedicated chef.

TABASCO SAUCE

This hot-pepper sauce is another seasoning that must be used with considerable discretion. A little is fine, imparts a real flavor and blends well with other essences, but too much is terrible. it does, however, have a definite place on the seasoning shelf. Many chefs prefer it to cayenne or chili pepper for this form of seasoning.

MUSTARD

Every seasoning shelf should have both dry and prepared mustard, of course. In most dishes the dry mustard is given in the recipe for a sound reason — the strength of dry mustard is known, and can be measured, whereas most prepared mustards vary in strength. If you happen to visit a good gourmet food mart, it would be interesting to invest in a few of the foreign prepared mustards, such as those turned out by Spanish, Italian, German and French manufacturers. You will find them quite different to the American prepared mustards, which are blends.

CHUTNEY

Although essentially a condiment, chutney is also used as a seasoning agent is some dishes. Some salad dressings, for example, call for the use of chopped chutney, and it provides an added and unusual tang to many dishes. So far as I am concerned, Major Grey's is the only one made.

WORCESTERSHIRE SAUCE

This sauce, also a blend of several herbs and spices, is another "tang" agent in cooking, and many recipes call for its use in moderation.

HORSERADISH

Here is another "condiment" that is occasionally employed as a seasoning in cookery. The difficulty with this lies in obtaining a good product. Freshly ground horseradish to which a bit of vinegar has been added is a fine seasoning, but not many kitchens are equipped to grind the root properly. A few food houses bottle *pure* horseradish which, if kept tightly sealed in a cool place, retains its honest flavor. The majority of the bottled horseradishes, for some strange reason, contain turnip as well as the hot root, and are far from satisfactory. If you are equipped to grind and bottle your own, fine. Otherwise you must accept second best.

13

The Importance of Wine

IT WOULD be impossible to overemphasize the importance of wine in cooking.

The opposition, if any exists, could not argue against the use of wine on the basis of expense or additional effort. The amount of wine used in the preparation of almost any dish adds but a few cents to the cost, and it calls for no additional effort.

On the credit side of the ledger, there are many arguments that can be advanced for using wine, especially in the cooking of game. In the first place, it enhances the flavor of the dish to a degree that those who do not use it would not believe possible. In a few of the dishes prepared with wine you get a *hint* of the fragrance of the wine itself, but in the majority you find it merely improves the flavor and even the texture of the food. If you *must* have proof, you can obtain it quite easily. Prepare one of the recipes in this book with the wine recommended, then prepare the same food without it. Conviction is certain.

The proper use of herbs and wine in American cookery is in its infancy, except in the older, finer restaurants. In recent years both wine and herbs are being used with greater frequency in home kitchens. It is surprising how many family cooks first experimented with herbs and wine when they were having guests to dine and wanted to make a good impression. Henceforth, both came into common use for ordinary family cooking. Even the cheaper cuts of meat, it was found, became not only palatable but delicious with the addition of a hint of herbs and a splash of wine.

Many of the recipes in this book are American in application, but foreign in origin, and it is quite apparent that some of them have been toned down to the American palate. In a number of instances, I believe, this has resulted in a certain improvement rather than a depreciation. I have collected recipes from a large part of North and South America, Europe, Africa and part of the Middle East. It is surprising how many of the recipes picked up in Wyoming and Illinois are duplicated, with a few minor changes, by those found in Hungary and Algeria.

It is not necessary to use "vintage" wines in cookery, but neither can you resort to the mass-production cheap wines. We have two really fine wine "provinces" in this country — California and New York. There are vintners in both these states who produce wines as fine in bouquet and flavor as any produced in Europe. Not all types can be duplicated in these states, of course, and our fortified wines are not yet equal to the best of Spain and Portugal, but both California and New York vintners (some of them) offer truly fine table wines. There is another advantage to be found in selecting a good American wine. It will cost you about one half what you would pay for a wine of similar quality produced in Europe. There is another factor that many do not consider when they decide to splurge on an expensive imported wine. That is, several of the really fine European wines *will not travel*. In their own sphere they are fine, but they cannot stand up under the rigors of transportation. This is especially true of several of the Italian wines, which are nectar when drunk on the margins of their districts, and vinegar when they arrive on the American table. A few of the French and German wines are equally touchy. Some recover after careful storage for long periods, some never do.

Wine drinking has been so badly misrepresented in this country that many are afraid to serve wine to guests in fear of being "wrong." The theory that you *must* serve a white wine with fish and poultry and a red wine with beef and veal is sheer stupidity. It is true that certain wines find greater harmony with certain types of food, but if you find a type of wine you like there is no reason why it cannot be served with fish, poultry, beef or any other meat. It must be admitted, however, that few red wines should be chilled, and few white wines served at room temperature. This, of course, is because of the nature of the wine rather than its color.

Many American households have settled upon the rosé wine as an all-round answer to the wine problem, and in many instances they have made a sound choice. The average rosé is neither too dry nor too sweet for the average palate, and it harmonizes well with almost any food, hot or cold. The finest of these rosé wines, in my opinion, is Tavel, but such is the tendency of the average American to go overboard that Tavel is now difficult to find. There is a rosé produced by a California vintner, Almaden, that I consider to be one of the finest available, regardless of price.

For the benefit of those who are interested in finding sound wines, at prices well within any household budget, I will list a few of the California and New York vintners who are more interested in turning out a fine wine than in making a quick turnover. Beaulieu (Cal.) — Louis Martini (Cal.) — Almaden (Cal.) — Paul Masson (Cal.) — Novitiati (Cal.) — Widmer (N.Y.) — Taylor (N.Y.) — Urbana (N.Y.) There are, of course, several others, but these vintners offer several "types," including Riesling, Chablis, rosé, Sauterne, claret, Burgundy, Barbera, Cabernet, and champagne. You would be surprised to know how many amateur wine experts, unconcerned with price, serve American wines in preference to imported wines on their own tables.

In the matter of Madeira, Marsala and sherry, only relatively small amounts are used in cookery, and I am convinced that the imported products are superior, with the exception of a few sherries. The Widmer sherry, for example, is as fine a cooking sherry as you could want. Most of the better California "brandies" (cognac types) are satisfactory for cooking, and Laird's applejack can be substituted for Calvados. The English consume most of the world's supply of port, and I have yet to hear an English port fancier who had a good word for American port, regardless of vintner. The same holds true of cordials and liqueurs. The finest are produced by foreign companies that have been turning out their specialized products for more than a hundred years.

There are but two things that set game apart from domestic meats — flavor and texture. Wine of a certain type and in limited quantities brings out the full flavor and improves the texture of almost any item of game, and the cook who ignores this fails to do justice to the dishes he prepares, or to the palates of those who partake.

14

Culinary Equipment

THOSE WHO ENJOY good food and take pleasure in its preparation (and
their ranks include the professional as well as amateur chefs) insist upon
having the proper culinary equipment.

By "proper culinary equipment" I do not mean the assortment of elec-
trical gadgets which are now available. Many of these motor-driven cutters,
choppers, blenders, hullers, de-stringers, de-seeders and similar pieces of
machinery are of real value in the restaurant kitchen, but few of them are
vital to the average home kitchen.

There are, however, certain specific items of equipment that are vital to
the proper preparation of food. They are not expensive, they have long life,
yet they contribute greatly to the ease of preparation as well as to the ulti-
mate flavor. What is more, they broaden the scope of the cook to whom they
are made available.

I will list below the items which I consider basic, then touch on other items that are helpful but not absolutely essential.

1. Food chopper, with a minimum of three disc inserts — coarse, medium, fine.
2. Two large wooden spoons.
3. Wooden chopping bowl with single-bladed chopper.
4. One wooden mallet with ½-pound head.
5. One boning knife with carbon steel blade.
6. One standard "butcher" knife with heavy 1½ by 12 inch blade of carbon steel.
7. One oil stone (coarse on one side, fine on the other).
8. Two eight-inch-diameter sieves, coarse and fine.
9. One colander.
10. One ten-inch whisk.
11. One rotary beater.
12. One twelve-inch meat saw.
13. One grater (plastic).
14. One garlic press.
15. One lemon or lime press.
16. One pair of poultry shears.
17. Six fifteen-inch skewers.
18. One larding needle (medium).
19. Three mixing bowls, one-quart, two-quart, four-quart, *all* in stainless steel.
20. Four-inch darning needle.
21. Four glazed pottery casseroles, one-quart, two-quart, three-quart, and four-quart, all with covers.
22. One four-quart glazed pottery bean pot, with cover.
23. One Pyrex or glazed pottery (one-quart) saucepan, with cover.
24. Three skillets, six-inch, ten-inch, fifteen-inch (covers to fit).
25. Four cooking pots, one-quart, two-quart, four-quart, eight-quart.
26. One graduated measuring cup, marked for ¼, ½, ¾, and whole cup.
27. One set of measuring spoons, table-spoons, teaspoon, half-teaspoon, quarter-teaspoon.
28. One chafing dish (minimum 12-inch) with alcohol or Sterno heating unit.
29. One double boiler with rounded bottom on upper unit.
30. One mortar and pestle.

While some of the items listed above require no additional explanation, it may be helpful to amplify the reasons for others. I shall take up these items by number.

Numbers 5 and 6: Carbon steel is specified for a sound reason. This metal will take and hold better edge than the currently popular stainless steel blades. Meat should be *cut,* not hacked.

Number 10: A wire whisk is not intended to replace the rotary beater, but for stirring sauces over flame, and for blending fluids, it is an essential piece of equipment.

Number 12: The meat, or bone saw, while absent in many kitchens, is extremely valuable. An inexpensive metal frame saw, employing a twelve-inch hacksaw blade, is now available.

Number 16: Poultry shears will prove invaluable in any kitchen.

Number 17: Skewers, preferably of stainless steel, are necessary for preparing moose, venison, or elk "en brochette."

Number 18: The larding needle is *essential* for almost all game. A needle capable of handling a quarter-inch larding strip is adequate, but the needle should be at least 15 inches long.

Number 19: Stainless-steel mixing bowls are specified as there may be occasions when it is important to use them over flame.

Number 20: The four-inch darning needle, or sailmaker's needle, is necessary for sewing game birds.

Number 21: Glazed pottery casseroles are stipulated as they can also be used over direct heat, and *should* be used for the preparation of all dishes where long cooking over a low flame is required. If metal containers are used for this purpose there will be many instances in which the metal will affect the true flavor.

Number 23: The small Pyrex or glazed pottery saucepan is *vital* for the preparation of *all* sauces that are to be simmered for any length of time. Many such sauces will take on a metallic flavor if prepared in metal containers.

Number 24: Skillets offer some basis for argument. Those who are willing to make a higher investment in culinary equipment will find heavy copper, tinned inside, provides the perfect answer. Today several manufacturers are turning out heavy iron skillets with a thick glaze. While not inexpensive, these are excellent, and have the additional advantage that they can be used for serving, as they are offered in several attractive colors. The heavy iron skillet after proper "curing" is inexpensive, and actually preferred by many. They should be rubbed with lard or vegetable oil and placed in a 400-degree oven, then wiped out with paper, oiled, and returned to the oven. Proper curing requires eight or ten trips to the oven. When washing the cured skillet, no abrasive should be used. The interior will be carbon-black, which is "as it should be." Personally, I prefer the above to the various stainless-steel skillets now on the market.

Number 25: The cooking pots mentioned can be of any metal desired, although I prefer those in stainless steel. The eight-quart pot may seem huge, but it will be used on countless occasions.

Number 28: A chafing dish is no longer an expensive item of equipment. Wrought-iron bases, while not as showy as those in copper or brass, are just as effective, and chafing dishes in lined copper are now available at very moderate prices.

Number 30: A small mortar and pestle, four or five inches in diameter, can be had in hardwood or porcelain and at a low cost. They are extremely valuable for blending herbs.

In addition to the basic equipment listed, there are a few of the new electric gadgets that could be listed as "helpful but not vital." Among these is the Waring mixer or blender, which is a definite asset to any chef, amateur or professional. If I could have but one piece of electric kitchen equipment, this is the one I would choose. It is extremely helpful in the blending of sauces, salad dressings, and for blending any liquids in small quantities. What is more, it converts heavy cream to sweet butter in a few seconds.

The electric mixer or beater is also a welcome addition to the kitchen equipment, especially as many of those now available have attachments that make a multi-purpose item.

The electric spit has, as a result of increased demand and competition, become available at a price that any amateur chef can

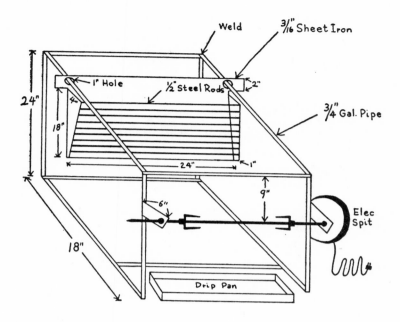

afford. A friend of mine, lacking a kitchen hearth, has evolved a portable spit and grill that can be stored in the basement or garage when not in use. In mild weather it can be placed on an old table on the porch, and in inclement weather pushed inside the fireplace in the living room. He places a 2½ by 2½ foot square of asbestos fiber board beneath it. Any local tinker with a welding outfit can make you one just like it. He paid a local sheet-metal shop $16 for his.

Another item that is extremely handy is the so-called "patent baster." This resembles a king-size eye dropper, with a stainless-steel tapered tube and a large rubber bulb. This gadget permits rapid and effective basting.

EQUIVALENTS

1 cup	½ pint	16 tablespoons
2 cups	16 ounces	1 pint
4 cups	1 quart	—
3 teaspoons	1 tablespoon	—
4 tablespoons	¼ cup	—
1 pinch	under ⅛ teaspoon	—
Breadcrumbs	1 cup	3 ounces
Butter	2 cups	1 pound
Butter	¼ pound	8 tablespoons
Cheese (cottage)	1 cup	½ pound
Cheese (grated)	1 cup	¼ pound
Corn meal	3 cups	1 pound
Cream	1 cup	½ pint
Egg (yolks)	1 cup	16 yolks
Flour	1 cup	¼ pound
Nuts (chopped)	1 cup	¼ pound
Oils (vegetable)	1 cup	7 ½ ounces
Rice (uncooked)	1 cup	½ pound
Rice (uncooked)	1 cup	3 to 3 ½ cups cooked
Spices (powdered)	1 ounce	4 tablespoons
Sugar (brown	1 cup	⅜ pound
Sugar (granulated)	1 cup	½ pound
Lemon (juiced)	2-3 tablespoons	—
Orange (juiced)	6-8 tablespoons	—

METRIC CONVERSION CHART

VOLUME		METRIC EQUIVALENT
1 tablespoon	=	14.7 cc (*cubic centimeters*)
1 teaspoon	=	4.9 cc
½ cup	=	118.3 cc
1 cup	=	236.7 cc
1 fluid ounce	=	29.5 cc
8 fluid ounces	=	236.7 cc
1 quart	=	1 liter (*approximate*) 946 milliliter
1 gallon	=	3¾ liters (*approximate*) 3785 milliliter

WEIGHT | |
---|---|---
1 dry ounce | = | 28.3 grams
1 pound | = | .454 kilograms

TO CONVERT

Ounces to grams: multiply the number of ounces by 28.35

Grams to ounces: multiply grams by .035

GAME FREEZING LIMIT

NAME	MAXIMUM TIME
Coot	4 months
Dove	5 months
Duck	4 months
Elk	12 months
Goose	4 months
Grouse	6 months
Hare	10 months
Liver	
Big Game	3 months
Small Game	4 months
Birds	4 months
Moose	12 months
Pheasant	6 months
Pigeon	6 months
Quail	6 months
Rabbit	10 months
Snipe	7 months
Squirrel	10 months
Turkey	8 months
Venison	10 months
Woodcock	7 months

Index